Bivocational

Ministry

Bivocational

Ministry

Field Notes for
Congregations
and Ministers

Kristen Plinke Bentley

chalice
PRESS

Print: 9780827203419

EPUB: 9780827203426

EPDF: 9780827203433

ChalicePress.com

Printed in the United States of America

For my parents, Barbara A. Plinke
and
John F. "Fritz" Plinke

Contents

The publication of *Bivocational Ministry* is supported in part by a gift from Higher Education & Leadership Ministries (HELM) of the Christian Church (Disciples of Christ). HELM recognizes congregational leadership takes many forms, including those who see ministry as a calling that lives alongside other employment in their lives. As a proud supporter of *Bivocational Ministry*, HELM is able to expand and continue its work of bringing students and resources together. To learn more about HELM and its mission, visit helmdisciples.org.

Acknowledgements

This book would not exist without the many people who have spoken with me about their experiences with bivocational ministry—either as ministers or church members. Many of them were eager to speak of their experiences "being bivocational" because they want to help others know more about a model of ministry that they have found valuable to them and their congregations. I am indebted to them for their willingness to talk with me about their personal experiences in ministry as well as their love for the congregations where they lead and worship.

Lilly Endowment Inc. has provided support for the bivocational ministry research at Lexington Theological Seminary since 2014. Their support included generous grant funding as well as experienced guidance through the coordination programs for their Economic Challenges Facing Future Ministers Initiative and Thriving in Ministry Initiative. This support and guidance provided many opportunities for engagement with theological educators, clergy, and laity interested in bivocational ministry and the economic challenges faced by clergy and congregations in North America.

Appreciation is due to many people who have supported the project of learning about bivocational ministry, including colleagues and students at Lexington Theological Seminary, where I have been privileged to work since 2014. Countless interactions have helped me learn about bivocational ministry and contributed to what is contained in the pages of this book. As partners in the LTS research project since its inception, the Christian Church in Kentucky provided significant support. I am grateful for those who have served as regional minister during this time, Greg Alexander, Dean Phelps and Donald K. Gillett, II, as well as for Lon Oliver and Rachel Nance Woehler, who both bring deep interest and experience in supporting bivocational ministers and the congregations they serve. I also am grateful for those who have provided helpful support in the process writing of this book. In May 2023 I joined the Writing Table program hosted by Eileen Campbell-Reed, and my participation in those weekday sessions, as well as coaching and advice from her, have helped strengthen my writing habits and skills. In addition, I am grateful to Sharyn Dowd and Carol Ruthven for their friendship and their willingness to provide feedback on what I have written and to engage in sustained conversation around ministry and the model of bivocational ministry. More than anyone else, I am grateful to Charisse L. Gillett, the president of LTS, for her role in hiring me to work at LTS on this research project and for relentlessly encouraging me to share what I was learning wherever I could, including writing this book.

I'm always grateful for my family members, their encouragement, and the many ways they have filled my life with love and adventure. I am grateful to my daughter, Kathryn Bentley Fetter, for her insights and feedback about early drafts of sections of this book. Most of all, I appreciate my husband, Perry Bentley, for his encouragement to "get it done" and for sharing insights from his expertise in accounting and law in connection with congregational ministry. Such insights from him have been helpful throughout my years of ministry, and their influence is seen in the content of chapter 5.

Great thanks go to the leadership and staff of Chalice Press for making this book possible. I especially appreciate the editorial staff and Brad Lyons, who helped cast a vision for the shape this book could take.

INTRODUCTION

Rev. Roberta Brown puts the car key in the ignition then sits back and takes a deep breath. Before driving away from the graveside, she looks down at the handwriting in the notebook on her lap—the words she has just prayed. She hopes they helped Gary Hill's bereaved family. She looks out the window and notices that the family has already gone, that only the cemetery workers are left, re-filling the grave with earth.

Roberta is tired. Over the past few days she has spent hours in the hospital, met with the family to talk about the funeral, and grieved on her own when she was back home. Both his family and the congregation will miss Elder Gary Hill. He had been a lifelong servant of the church. That he was really gone is hard for her to imagine; recalling his habit of pulling his pencil and his "to do" list out of his shirt pocket, she whispers, "Well done, good and faithful servant."

As Roberta prepares to leave the cemetery, the next few days loom in her mind. Her boss has been understanding and has given her time off from her other job for this funeral. But bright and early tomorrow morning she will hit the highway for a long-planned business trip. Mentally she ticks off what she needs to do next: pack her suitcase, review materials for the upcoming business meetings, and go over childcare plans with her mother for while she is gone. Startled to remember she'll be back home only late on Saturday afternoon, she wonders, "How in the world will I find time to finish the work on Sunday's sermon?"

Roberta Brown is one of thousands of ministers across the United States who pastor a congregation while also employed outside the church. Such "bivocational ministry" has long been practiced in the United States among Protestant churches, especially in rural areas and in African American congregations, as well as in other racial and ethnic communities and among immigrant and refugee communities. Furthermore, bivocational ministry remains a central strategy for planting new churches.

Since the economic downturn in 2008, increasing attention has focused on bivocational ministry as a viable financial strategy to support congregational ministry. Many churches cannot afford full compensation and benefits to support a minister. And many ministers cannot support themselves or their households on what congregations can afford to pay them. They need supplemental income. In the bivocational ministry model, ministers earn that supplemental income by working outside the church; this approach contributes to financial stability for both the ministers and the churches they serve.

How many ministers in the U.S. pastor while employed outside their congregations is unclear. One recent national survey estimated that one-third of congregations in the U.S. have lead ministers who also hold other employment.[1] In addition to those lead ministers, others are serving congregations in roles such as associate minister, youth minister, or music minister. Even without a definitive count, bivocational ministry is clearly a significant part of the current ministerial landscape. This model of ministry provides crucial help at a time when many congregations face economic challenges.

As a strategy for financial support for Christian ministry and mission, it has been around for millennia, with roots extending to the New Testament and the earliest days of the church. According to Acts 18:3, the apostle Paul supported himself as a tentmaker or leatherworker while he ministered in Corinth. Acts 20:34 quotes him as stating that he worked with his own hands to support himself and his coworkers. Paul confirmed this practice himself when he wrote to the church in Corinth (1 Cor. 9:3–18), and he referred again to a practice of supporting himself and others when ministering at Thessalonica (1 Thess. 2:9) and at Ephesus (1 Cor. 4:12).

---

[1] Chaves et al., *Congregations in 21st Century America: National Congregations Study* 2021, 4, https://sites.duke.edu/ncsweb/files/2022/02/NCSIV_Report_Web_FINAL2.pdf.

What Do We Mean by "Bivocational Ministry"?

I first encountered the term "bivocational" when I was a pastor of a small church. Though not bivocational myself at the time, I knew of ministers who were. I was serving in a church and was being paid for about twenty hours of work each week. I neither *needed* to get another job (because I had a working spouse who provided enough income—including health insurance— for our household), nor did I *want* another job (because we had school-aged children at home and my hands were full). I knew other ministers in the area who were pastoring while teaching or pastoring while running a farm or family business.

I became more familiar with the term in 2013 when Lexington Theological Seminary (LTS), my alma mater, invited me to lead a grant project that Lilly Endowment Inc. funded as part of its Economic Challenges Facing Future Ministers Initiative. The project's goal was to address problems associated with mounting educational debt among people preparing for ministry within the Christian Church (Disciples of Christ) and to launch a research project to learn more about the experiences of bivocational ministers in Kentucky. In beginning to work on the project at LTS in 2014 while also serving a rural church in a neighboring county, I became a bivocational minister myself.

In the years since then, I have been privileged to turn much of my energy and attention to learning more about the experiences of bivocational ministers and the congregations they serve within the Christian Church. From 2014 to 2018 the work focused on congregations and ministers in Kentucky. That focus expanded in 2019 thanks to a grant from Lilly's Thriving in Ministry Initiative. This book's stories, conversations, and insights regarding bivocational ministry[2] are rooted in the research project supported by these two grants from Lilly Endowment, as well as in my own ministry experience.

That project entailed various research activities. In 2015 I sent a survey to Disciples of Christ ministers serving in Kentucky

---

[2] When giving names for ministers, lay people, and congregations in stories and conversations, I use pseudonyms, unless otherwise noted, to protect their privacy.

congregations. Of the 110 ministers who completed it, 40 percent served in bivocational arrangements. In the next three years I followed that with semi-structured interviews with pastors and lay leaders in Kentucky, with surveys of LTS students, and with various continuing education programs designed with bivocational ministers in mind. In 2023 I launched a second series of semi-structured interviews in congregations from diverse contexts within the Christian Church, this time outside of Kentucky. All these activities and the information they collected have informed this book. To date, the interviews have included ministers and lay leaders serving in twenty-four congregations.

The survey and interviews disclosed that people talk about bivocational ministry in many different ways. Some people admit with embarrassment that they used to think of bivocational ministry as "second-class" ministry. These folks typically had spent most of their lives in large, predominantly white churches and had never been around many bivocational ministers themselves. One day I met a pair of churchgoers who learned of the economic focus of the work I was doing. They spoke proudly of their "sacrificial" minister who had "never asked for a salary increase, like some others do," to which I replied: "Well, I hope [the minister has] some other source of income." Another person approached me at a regional assembly after learning about the project, saying: "Hello! I was bivocational before it was 'cool.'" He laughed and said he could tell me about some great experiences. I was all ears! I wanted to learn from those who had long-term experience of "being bivocational." Through listening to these different perspectives and experiences, I have learned a great deal.

I resonated with some of what interviewees told me. For example, other women in ministry reported being in part-time or bivocational positions because of parenting responsibilities or their lack of geographical mobility due to a spouse's employment. Yet interviews with women who had experiences different from mine reminded me how important it is to step outside personal frames of reference when seeking to understand others. As a minister who is a sixty-something, white, married, heterosexual woman, I have learned much from those whose age, race/ethnicity, marital status, or sexual/gender identity differs from mine. As expressed in this time-honored threefold formulation of human personhood, "every human person is in certain respects: (1) like all others, (2) like some others, and (3) like no other."[3] There are no one-size-fits-all stories of bivocational ministry.

In 2020 a profound realization led me to refine the way I defined bivocational ministry. Up to that point I had considered all bivocational ministers in Disciples congregations to be licensed, commissioned, or ordained ministers who were employed by the churches they served. However, in conversing with students in the newly developed Certificate in African American Ministry program at LTS in 2020, I learned that some of the bivocational ministers enrolled in that program were neither licensed, commissioned, nor ordained, nor were all of them paid employees of their congregations. Some were serving as pastors without being compensated, yet they understood that serving the church as a minister was their highest and best calling. This was an eye-opening realization for me and served as a much-needed corrective, particularly as I sought to expand the research project beyond Kentucky to engage more fully with the social, ethnic, and racial diversity of bivocational ministry. I revised the definition of a bivocational minister for this book and for the interviews launched in 2023 to be "individuals who serve as recognized ministers in a congregation and have paid employment outside that congregation." Though it is a better, more inclusive definition, it still doesn't answer all the questions.

Terminology

People use different terms to talk about this model of ministry, often interchangeably. Terms like "tentmaking," "covocational ministry," "multivocational ministry," and "bivocational ministry" emphasize different dimensions of the model. "Tentmaking" emphasizes the connection to the apostle Paul's evangelistic mission and work described in the New Testament; some people use it to refer to ministers who work to support themselves while working for the church without pay in order to maximize their

---

[3] Emmauel Y. Lartey, *In Living Color: An Intercultural Pastoral Care and Counseling*, 2nd ed. (Philadelphia: Jessica Kingsley Publishers, 2003), 34. Quoted from C. Kluckholm & H. Murray in *Personality in Nature, Society and Culture* (New York: Alfred Knoff, 1948).

missional and evangelistic impact. The terms "multivocational" and "covocational" reflect the meaning of Christian vocation within a model of ministry that is complex and diverse. After all, to many people "bivocational" means "a minister with two jobs," when in fact many ministers have multiple jobs outside the church they serve. Some people regard the term "bivocational" as giving inadequate honor to "vocation" as a call from God to ministry. Truly, in one way of thinking, all of us who are Christians could say we are "bivocational" because we fulfill our baptismal calling—our "vocation"— as we serve in the name of Jesus Christ both inside the church and in the world outside the church in our daily lives.

In this book I use the traditional term "bivocational" because it communicates a general sense of what it means: ministers who have paid work outside a congregation. It is also the term ministers used early on in the project to identify themselves. In 2014, I met with some folks who were serving as bivocational ministers in Kentucky to talk about their experiences. They not only used the term "bivocational," but they also said quite emphatically that they did not want to be called "part-time" ministers. They simply did not think "part time" was the best way to describe their model of ministry, which often included a variety of duties including attending meetings and engaging in pastoral care during the week while also preparing for weekly worship and preaching and other duties. They made the case that they were fully engaged in ministry in ways that were not communicated with the term "part time."

However, others embraced the term "part time," and those ministers shared similarities with bivocational ministers. For instance, ministers engaged to work part time (usually fewer than thirty hours per week) in congregations, like those who are bivocational, help churches address the economic challenges of providing full compensation and employment benefits for them. Also, when part-time ministers work fewer hours per week, they have less time to accomplish ministry tasks, leaving openings for increased lay participation in the ministry of the church. In addition, serving part time can help make more space in ministers' lives for other relationships, such as with friends and family members. One female bivocational minister who also has a school-aged child at home expressed a preference for working part time, saying: "I want the right of refusal. I want to be able to say 'no' ... to balance the areas in my life. So part-time [work] buys me freedom." These part-time ministers supplement what the church pays them with income from other sources, such as investment or retirement funds, the employment of another household member, or their own employment beyond the church. Interestingly, in the 2015 LTS survey, 60 percent of all ministers (including those who identified as bivocational) reported that income from a spouse's employment contributed to their household income. Many times such spousal employment also provides health insurance coverage for the minister and household.

Who Are Bivocational Ministers?

While it may be tempting to view bivocational ministry simply as a subset of part-time ministry, there are ministers working in what they describe as full-time and fully funded ministry who also do paid work outside of their church. Aren't they bivocational? What about those who have two (or more) ministry positions (one in and one out of a particular congregation), including those ministers who serve more than one congregation?[4] Are they bivocational? I think so, and I see them as a special subset of bivocational ministry. What about those congregational ministers who for seasons of their lives participate in unpaid and labor-intensive occupations outside the congregation, such as parenting young children at home, caring for adults, and doing intensive unpaid ministry outside the church? While I don't consider them bivocational unless they also have paid work outside the church, they share similar challenges. (Check out the diagram on page 8 to see some definitional boundaries. You might find yourself wishing to adjust the diagram.) There's diversity in bivocational ministry that doesn't fit neatly into definitions and categories. The significant challenge for bivocational ministers, in contrast to those who identify as part time or full time, comes from the additional responsibilities related to their paid employment outside the congregation.

---

[4] The practice of one minister serving two or more small churches is common in some denominations, such as The United Methodist Church.

Who are the Bivocational Ministers?*

Some bivocational ministers are contracted to work forty+ hours/week in a church with full compensation and benefits and also employed outside the church (e.g. as a part-time or contract employee or freelancer).

Part-time Ministers — ministers who are engaged for thirty hours or fewer hours work/week in a congregation. Some of them are bivocational ministers.

Bivocational Ministers — ministers who are engaged to work in a congregation while also employed outside the congregation they serve.

Some bivocational ministers work in one or more other paid ministry positions (e.g. a regional ministry role, a chaplain, or yoked to another congregation).

Ministers with Unfunded Work outside the congregation. There are many ministers, some of whom are bivocational, who also are doing labor intensive unpaid work (i.e. mission volunteers, parents of young children, caregivers for adults in their families).

* This diagram shows overlapping relationships. The sizes of the circles do not represent numbers in the populations.

What makes ministers "bivocational" is that they serve a congregation, week in and week out, while also working for pay outside the church. The ministers serve in a variety of capacities in congregations and in a variety of outside jobs. Many are employed outside in one full-time job, some hold one or more part-time positions, some are self-employed, and some work for hourly wages. In some cases the work outside the congregation is another type of ministry position, such as working in a denomination's regional office, as a chaplain, or even as a pastor of another congregation. In these cases there may be a helpful overlap in the positions, one that may provide more flexibility for all involved. All in all, these ministers are employed in the wider community in a variety of roles—as administrators, artists, bankers, business owners, chaplains, elected officials, factory workers, farmers, financial advisors, government workers, house cleaners, lawyers, teachers, and Uber drivers.

Why Bivocational Ministry?

One thing I noticed when interviewing ministers and laypeople in Kentucky is that those in bivocational arrangements think in a variety of different ways about their ministry model and the financial stability it allows them and their churches. These ways represent:

- A Sign of the Times
- The Cutting Edge of the Future
- The Way We've Always Done Ministry

Each of these narrative themes recognizes that the congregation has limited financial resources, but each one understands those limitations and their relation to bivocational ministry differently. In each of these three narratives, "being bivocational" contributes to improved financial stability even though it does not solve all financial woes the minister and/or the congregation faces. The congregations can afford their ministers, thanks to the ministers' income from employment outside the church; and the ministers can afford to serve the congregations, despite the congregations' limited financial resources.

A SIGN OF THE TIMES: A RESPONSE TO DECLINE

In the "A Sign of the Times" narrative, the church understands bivocational ministry as a response to decline. Churches with this mindset typically have been experiencing loss of membership and financial resources and are employing a bivocational minister as a response to that loss. Many of these congregations are predominantly white congregations in decline. They may be hopeful about bivocational ministry in some ways, but they see the shift as one more sign that their congregation is declining and possibly moving toward closure as a church. These congregations have challenging adjustments to make as they transition to ministry with a bivocational minister.

THE CUTTING EDGE OF THE FUTURE: A STRATEGY TO GROW

In "The Cutting Edge of the Future" narrative, congregations still face economic challenges, but they regard the bivocational model as part of a strategy for ministry and mission as they start something new. These congregations see having a minister with a "day job" or "side hustle" as a promising way to jump-start something new and missional. It could mean they are a new church start or an established congregation in the process of transforming its way of ministry.

THE WAY WE'VE ALWAYS DONE MINISTRY: A CONTINUATION OF PRACTICE

In "The Way We've Always Done Ministry" narrative, there are still financial challenges, but those challenges are not new. Churches with this narrative in mind cannot remember a time when their ministers did not have other jobs outside the church. For them, bivocational ministry is not a sign of decline, but rather a feature of their congregation's resilience. Some even proclaim it as the superior model of ministry and cite its biblical connections. Most rural congregations and most historically African American congregations fit this narrative. They have shaped much of their identity and their practices of ministry around bivocational arrangements. One retired African American minister who served in bivocational contexts for more than thirty years told me: "I never heard the term 'bivocational' growing up. ... I always heard our pastors referred to as 'our pastor,' period. In my opinion, the terms 'bivocational' or 'part-time' were imposed upon African American clergy. ... I dare say, most African American pastors see their ministry as their 'highest calling,' and they work outside the call in order to fulfill it."

Call and Response

Ministers "become bivocational" via different routes and for different reasons. Some pursue theological education anticipating they will serve the church in a bivocational arrangement after graduation and ordination. Some who ended up taking this route commented on their sense of call:

- "There is a wider calling—not just to the church, but also the world. ... The job you have every day is your ministry; your church service also is your ministry."

- "Small, mostly rural churches deserve a quality of ministry and service the same as larger congregations. I can financially afford to do that."

- "I expected to be a pastor while continuing in my previous career before seminary; I thought combining the two would provide more opportunities to serve God."

However, quite a few ministers who serve in bivocational arrangements did not pursue theological education intending to become bivocational ministers. While not an exhaustive list, some of the various paths to bivocational ministry include:

- sensing a call to ministry, beginning to serve a congregation, then later pursuing theological education and formation for ministry

- responding to a particular congregation's needs while employed in the area, discerning a call to ministry, then pursuing education to become a commissioned or ordained minister

- shifting *to* bivocational arrangements after seeking or serving in fully funded positions in churches for reasons such as the minister's lack of geographical mobility, inability to land a fully funded position, or inability to live on the amount their current church pays them and consequently needing to find another job

- shifting *away from* fully funded ministry due to dissatisfaction with their previous ministry, because of new interests in their lives, or because being bivocational fits better with their lives

The various paths and motivations that lead people to become bivocational ministers are part of the complexity of bivocational ministry, with some coming to it with more intention than others. Regardless of the direction or the path of approach, such ministers face similar challenges.

Hopes for the Book

This book invites those who love the church to explore what helps congregations and ministers involved in bivocational ministry to thrive. No doubt readers come from different places of interest and experience related to bivocational ministry. You may come with a long history of "being bivocational" with interest about how others are doing it. You may be in the process of considering a shift to, or newly engaged with, the model of bivocational ministry and may be looking for insight and help. Or you may be curious about the model, having always been in congregational settings where fully funded ministers work only in the church.

However you come to the book, in it you will find a storehouse of experiences about bivocational ministry. Each chapter contains numerous stories of bivocational ministers and the congregations they serve. Together, they explore benefits and drawbacks to bivocational ministry and make recommendations for ways bivocational ministry might be strengthened. Questions for reflection and discussion follow each chapter, in hopes of sparking conversations about how bivocational ministers and congregations might grow and support each other to thrive in ministry.

I hope that ministers, laypeople, and congregations engaged in bivocational ministry will feel *seen, heard,* and *respected* through what is shared in this book and that the stories, insights, and reflections about bivocational ministry, as well as the questions for discussion and reflection, generate meaningful and hopeful conversations. Although bivocational ministry has been widely practiced in the U.S., for much of its history it has been overlooked or oversimplified. It is a significant segment of the present ministry landscape and will be so in the future. If conversations sparked by what is shared in this book could contribute to more affirmation and less fear of bivocational ministry, it could lay some groundwork to strengthen support for bivocational ministry as well. Much can be done to support more fully the ministers and congregations engaged in it.

At the 2023 General Assembly of the Christian Church in Louisville, Kentucky, a banner stating "Ministry Thrives with Support" topped a wooden trellis behind a table of resources in the exhibit hall. Vines with felt leaves were woven into the trellis. As people visited the table, they were invited to jot down something on a slip of paper about what support helps ministry to thrive. Their notes were added to the trellis like "beams of support" for ministry. It was an interactive way to help people identify important sources and systems of support for ministry in all contexts. People added things like:

- affordable theological education
- clergy peer groups
- experienced mentors who can relate
- guidance for lay leaders
- helping bivocational ministers with resources
- resources for smaller churches
- strong support groups

The list was a good start. Each of us could probably add more to it, from things we already have in place to those we still need. Congregations and ministers in all kinds of settings find they are more likely to thrive in ministry when given support.

I hope that this book can be part of imagining what a trellis of support for bivocational ministry might look like. Ministers like Rev. Roberta Brown, whom we met at the beginning of this introduction, are doing good work while facing significant challenges. We left Roberta as she was leaving the cemetery and thinking about how to find time to finish her sermon for Sunday while also taking care of her responsibilities to her other job and her family. Like other bivocational ministers, Roberta would benefit from a trellis of support.

The Disciples of Christ as a Case Study

The story I am telling about bivocational ministry in the Disciples of Christ in this book could be considered an extended case study. The Christian Church's history, congregation-centered polity, and participation in mainline Protestantism make it a good place from which to view dimensions of bivocational ministry in the twenty-first-century United States. Why?

First, because it is a U.S.-born tradition. Many Disciples of Christ congregations trace their roots to traveling preachers/planters of the nineteenth-century Stone Campbell Tradition. Like bivocational ministers today, those preacher/planters were employed outside the church.

Second, because like others within the Stone Campbell Tradition and churches in the free church tradition, Disciples have a polity that understands local congregations as the primary expression of the community of faith. This means that Disciples congregations have a sense of independence in the way they order their ministry, in how they respond to challenges, and in whom they nurture and call to be congregational leaders. It means that they decide whom to call as ministers as well as how to compensate them. As a result, within the Christian Church there's a wide range of ministerial compensation, and this means that some ministers suffer economically due to insufficient pay, lack of health insurance, and access to other benefits.

While the Christian Church has a well-developed Search and Call process, ministers who are not geographically mobile are often called to congregations through other processes. Those processes which congregations employ vary and sometimes resemble the secular job market, with congregations setting the rate of compensation and ministerial candidates looking for positions with better pay. When viewed bluntly, congregations can look like secular employers in that they have the power to "hire and fire."

Third, because like others within mainline Protestantism, Disciples of Christ have a historic emphasis of an educated clergy and have long viewed the M.Div. degree as the primary avenue to prepare for ordained ministry. In the late twentieth century, many in the mainline began to see that the educational debt for those preparing for ministry and the employment possibilities for spouses related to the geographic constraints of ministers' locations were significant economic challenges. They also became increasingly aware both that many people who sensed a call to ministry did not have access to graduate seminary education and that many congregations were unable to attract (or afford) seminary-trained, ordained ministers. Seeking to address these concerns, in August 2011 the General Assembly of the Christian Church approved a seminary track and a new apprentice track preparation for ordained ministry and clarified processes for commissioned ministry. The combined challenges for the Disciples of Christ and the ways they are being addressed help to clarify issues that affect congregations and ministers in bivocational arrangements.

CHAPTER 1

Bivocational Ministry Is Good for the Church

Along a busy two-lane highway in rural Kentucky stands a solid, red brick church. It's been at this same spot for 160 years, founded by an evangelist with the Stone Campbell Movement who also was a local farmer. Except for a few years in the 1990s, when the predominantly white church experimented with a fully funded minister, it has been led by evangelists or ministers who have had other sources of income to supplement whatever the church paid them. The current pastor is an ordained female minister who lives and teaches in a town a little over fifteen miles away.

Today drivers speed through this section of road and barely glimpse the church and its grounds, a cluster of smallish houses, a neglected cemetery, and a building that houses a sandwich shop—all that's left of a once promising "crossroads community" established in the eighteenth century. In its heyday it was a village with three churches, its own post office, a short-line railroad depot, its own school, and a variety of small businesses including general merchandise stores that provided almost anything one needed in a typical day. Some people in the church still tell stories of those days.

This church is the most visible point in a community that could have been named "Mighthavebeenville,"[5] a place reshaped by time. Changes in the surrounding county after World War II greatly shifted living and transportation patterns. In the 1950s consolidation of services closed both their community school and their post office. In what now seems like the blink of an eye,

___

[5] Shannon Jung, *Rural Ministry: The Shape of the Renewal to Come* (Nashville, TN: Abingdon Press, 1998), 75–86.

daily occasions on which people gathered and greeted each other disappeared. Then, in the 1960s, a major interstate interchange was constructed five miles down the road. With the new transportation so convenient, the short-line railroad stop was no longer needed.

The church's building and grounds are used not only for Sunday ministry but also for community gatherings including birthday parties, baby showers, anniversary celebrations, small weddings, and receptions. Some nonprofit groups in the area also meet in the facilities, which church members recently renovated with a modernized kitchen and accessible restrooms.

On Sundays around thirty people gather for in-person worship. Like many other churches, this one took a hit during the COVID-19 pandemic, and the congregation is still working its way back from that. The church hosts a regular Bible study and uses its weekly tithes and offerings to pay the church's bills and support mission projects. In between Sundays the church people live, work, and serve in the area.

Less than four miles down the road and around a corner stands another red brick church, part of a different Protestant tradition. It was built on a twenty-acre parcel of land purchased in the 1870s by formerly enslaved people to establish an African American community. That community and church still include people descended from those founders, some of whom were celebrated civil rights activists in the county.

This church property includes a covered picnic pavilion and a cemetery. Each week around forty people gather for Sunday worship and Bible study, hold a weekday study, and host regular community and leadership development activities. Evangelists and ministers who have led this church over the years all have had other jobs to supplement what the church provided. With the new lead minister, who is a seminary graduate, this church is trying something different. The minister serves the church as part of a recognized ministry team with his wife; while he does not have other employment, she does.

There are other churches down the roadways from these two. If a drone hovered over the entire county of 57,000 residents, it would see more than thirty churches. They are situated in a variety of locations: some at crossroads, some nestled in farmland, some on main streets and side streets of the county's towns. Some of their congregations meet in private homes, some in rented storefronts, and others in basements of church buildings they do not own. Some have similar back stories and theological views; others are dramatically different. Some are declining, some thriving, some closing their doors, and others just getting started. Many of these churches, except perhaps for the largest among them, are led by ministers who also have other jobs.

The drone's-eye view doesn't tell us everything, but it does give us a glimpse of the mixed ecology of the twenty-first-century ministry landscape. Like the cultivated field of 1 Corinthians 3:9, over the years these churches have been planted and watered by different evangelists and ministers. For many of them, their resilience is due, at least in part, to the leadership of ministers who also have worked for pay outside those churches.

Most Congregations in the U.S. Are Small

"Most congregations are small, but most people are in large congregations." When I came across this online statement about congregational life in the U.S., it took me a while to realize that both parts of the statement could be true. I looked for its source and read further into the National Congregations Study[6] to consider this apparent paradox. As I read on, it began to make sense. I thought of the immense size of two megachurches located close to where I live. According to this report, a minority of churches (9 percent of all congregations) are so large that they contain most of the churchgoers in the U.S. The vast majority (91 percent) of congregations are on the smaller side. In 2018–2019 the median congregation had only seventy regular participants, counting children and adults.[7] The report goes on to say that 75 percent of ministers serve those smaller congregations. Reflecting on the "seventy regular participants," I realized that most of the Disciples congregations at which I've interviewed bivocational ministers

---

[6] Chaves et al., National Congregations Study, 4, 10–11, https://sites. duke.edu/ncsweb/files/2022/02/NCSIV_Report_Web_FINAL2.pdf.
[7] Chaves et al., National Congregations Study, 10–11.

and laypeople fit into that category, with their average in-person worship attendance on Sundays ranging between twenty and eighty people. While not all are small, most are. They are part of the vast majority of congregations in the land, yet their presence is overshadowed by a minority of large churches.

Who Is the Ideal Minister?

Particularly in U.S. mainline Protestantism, for several decades the idea that every church should strive to have a "full-time" minister has been the norm. This ideal "full-time" minister would be a pastor/professional who "can do it all" and whose full focus would be on the congregation. Ideally, such a minister would be seminary-educated and ordained, with the congregation as their sole employer. In exchange, the congregation would provide compensation commensurate with full-time employment, including health insurance, retirement, and other benefits.

Writer and church leader Mark Edington describes this model of ministry as the "Standard Model." He explains that much of what is understood in mainline Protestantism related to the church, ministry, and congregational leadership—and the underlying economic arrangements—has been designed around this professional model of ministry.[8] It has been used as a "standard" against which other models of ministry, including the model of bivocational ministry, have been measured.

Yet that idea of ministry has never told the full story. While it works well in some situations and contexts, there have always been vital congregations led by ministers who do not fit that pattern. In addition, its dominance has sidelined other models of ministry. The focus on the one model has discouraged and misled congregations for which other models, such as bivocational ministry and part-time ministry, would be a better fit.

The dominance of the model of the full-time professional minister has contributed to what journalist and minister Jeffrey MacDonald calls a "full-time bias" in the church.[9] Perhaps this

---

[8] Mark Edington, *Bivocational: Returning to the Roots of Ministry* (New York: Church Publishing, 2018), 3–7.

[9] Jeffrey MacDonald, *Part-Time Is Plenty: Thriving without Full-time Clergy* (Louisville, KY: Westminster John Knox Press, 2020), 23–25.

bias explains why bivocational ministers early in the Lexington Theological Seminary research project rejected the term "part time" for their ministry. MacDonald wants to resist the stigma associated with part-time ministry, the stigma that presents such ministry as "half-hearted" or "less than serious."[10] In discussing the "full-time bias," he points out how the very term "full-time ministry" is misleading:

> Full-time refers to working forty of the 168 hours in a single week, yet it's valorized as if it were a complete commitment in contrast to, say, a part-timer who gives 18 percent of his/her entire week to a 30-hour job. In other words, everyone only gives a fraction of their lives to work, even those who are salaried and put in more than 40 hours.[11]

Commitment to church ministry is not measured by hours worked. The amount of time ministers spend each week in the church building does not equate to the quality of their ministry. Likewise, when ministers serve in "full-time positions," that does not mean they have given over their entire lives to that work. There are boundaries to be observed in ministry, even though ministers may occasionally be called out of bed in the middle of the night for an emergency. Some ministers insist "it's a 24/7 calling." Yet that may be an invitation to destructive overload when actually the "24/7 calling" is to be alive and loved by God. All ministers, including those who think of themselves as "full-time ministers," have permission to live personal lives that are themselves full. The lives of all ministers, like those of all people, belong to God; ministers are not "owned" by the church, even if paid a hefty salary.

Congregations of all shapes and sizes do well to recognize the commitment and dedication of all sorts of ministers. Ministers — whether they are called "bivocational," "part-time," or "full-time" — all have the capacity to love and lead with heart, spirit, mind, and strength wholly engaged with God's purposes. The ideal minister for any congregation is the person whom God has gifted in the way that helps that congregation serve God best in their situation and context.

---

[10] MacDonald, *Part-Time Is Plenty*, 26.
[11] MacDonald, *Part-Time Is Plenty*, 23–25.

Thankfully people are coming to recognize more fully that congregations benefit from different models to pursue vital ministry. People are coming to recognize that the story of ministry is bigger than that one model alone. Novelist Chimamanda Ngozi Adichie reminds us it is dangerous to rely on a single story to understand people and places. She states, "The single story creates stereotypes, and the problem with stereotypes is not that they are untrue, but that they are incomplete."[12] There is no "one-size-fits-all" story of ministry, and it is good to recognize the many stories of ministry, some of which challenge an ideal that has been standardized and dominant. When these many stories are told, a more complete picture of ministry emerges, one that includes bivocational ministry moving away from the sidelines as it receives renewed attention.

A Valuable Model

Pastors and lay leaders interviewed as part of the LTS research project believe in the value of bivocational ministry. In contrast to seeing it as "less than" other forms of ministry, they believe it has unique benefits. The ministers serve bivocationally because they are financially able to do so and because they know the needs of the congregations they serve. These ministers and layleaders indicate that bivocational ministry supports:

- financial stability for congregations
- financial stability and independence for ministers
- congregational ministry in contexts with access to fewer resources
- financially sustainable mission and ministry in new contexts
- collaborative ministry leadership in congregations by re-aligning relationships between ministers and laypeople

---

[12] Chimamanda Ngozi Adichie, "The Danger of a Single Story," TED Talks, 2008, video, 19:16, https://www.youtube.com/watch?v=LmjKUDo7gSQ

My interviews with congregations reveal that successful bivocational ministry relies on more than a minister having another job that helps to pay the bills. Success also involves collaboration within congregations and a sense of ministry that is shared rather than pastor-centered. The financial advantages that ministers' additional employment provides for congregations also affect the minister-congregation relationship and push against the misleading image of the pastor/professional who "can do it all." Although some congregations do it better than others, most are working toward ministry that is a shared endeavor.

A Different Dynamic

Indeed, bivocational ministry seems to empower and promote ministry that is shared by re-aligning the relationship between congregation and minister. Because ministers do not depend upon the congregation for their livelihood, their relationship with the congregation shifts to one of balance. This was most surprising to people in their first-time experience of bivocational ministry after previously having served congregations that had provided their entire livelihood. One such minister reflected that, intentionally or not, bivocational ministry "created a different orientation to the church and the whole financial aspect." He said: "I have really experienced what shared ministry is like. ... They don't look at me with the attitude of, 'Well, we hired *you* to do that.'" Both ministers and lay leaders indicated that because the congregation was not the minister's sole employer, the temptation to think of ministry as the job of the minister was reduced. A sense of mutual benefit is reflected in the key role lay leadership plays in congregations served by bivocational ministers. Ministers note success where strong lay leaders partner with them, especially with administration and pastoral care and even preaching.[13]

Another Story of the Church

The story (told earlier in this chapter) of the congregations in one county provided an overview of types of ministry, outlining

---

[13] Kristen Plinke Bentley, "Stability Amidst Turbulent Times: The Benefits of Bi-Vocational Ministry," *Colloquy Online,* Association of Theological Schools (May 2019), https://www.ats.edu/files/galleries/stability-amidst-turbulent-times-the-benefits-of-bi-vocational-ministry.pdf.

the role of bivocational ministry within the broader landscape of ministry. Let's turn now to a story of the role of bivocational ministry within one minister's life and the way it benefited the wider church.

Rev. Matthew reflects with gratitude on his more than thirty-five years as a bivocational minister. Now retired, he pastored several congregations in the Washington, D.C., area while also working in the banking profession. He looks back with some astonishment at how pastoral ministry unfolded for him.

Matthew grew up in a middle-class, white, churchgoing family and sensed a call to pastoral ministry in high school. "I had a very clear sense of call in the summer of my ninth-grade year ... at church camp," he said. Yet, regarding bivocational ministry, he said, "I planned to be a minister. ... The bivocational part was a bit more accidental."

After high school Matthew went to college, where particular people encouraged him to explore a variety of vocational opportunities. In 1970, his freshman year in college, the professor of his biology class noticed his academic progress and said to him: "I understand the ministry is where you want to go, but, you know, you really should think about how God's given you some abilities, and maybe you should use them." Matthew listened to this advice; he became a biology/chemistry major with a math minor and went on to graduate school to study physiology. Yet the call to ministry persisted, and Matthew transferred to a graduate theological seminary. One of his seminary teachers saw his interest in math shining through his seminary courses and encouraged him to apply for an internship in Washington, D.C. He took the advice and won an internship with AARP. He and his wife, Anne, moved to the D.C. area for the internship, and he took on a student church while continuing his seminary studies, which included an emphasis on pastoral counseling.

The church was very small, with eleven members and an annual budget of about $11,000. Matthew and Anne moved into the parsonage; Matthew pastored (for $100 a week), and Anne played piano for the church (she volunteered her services). Anne took on a full-time job, which provided their health insurance.

About that church, Matthew said, "They were incredibly loving people, and they loved their church and they loved anybody who walked within five hundred miles of their church." And so, after Matthew was ordained and after Anne had their first child, he stayed at the church and took care of their new son while Anne returned to her full-time job.

Then one day Anne came home from work and said she wanted to stop working and spend more time with their child. So Matthew went to the church board chairperson and told him: "I'm going to need to get a bigger church. I've got to get health insurance and take care of my family." The board chair (who was a banker) suggested another alternative. Matthew recounts: "He said, 'Wait ... things are really happening here. ... Why don't you get a job as a bank teller? You could do that because they're not allowed to be open on Saturday or Sunday, and we need you at night and we need you on weekends.'" So Matthew became a bank teller (at a different bank than where the board chairperson worked). "It turned out to be a very good move," he said. "I became a bivocational minister because of the birth of my son."

Matthew continued at that church for eight years. The combination of being a minister and a bank teller worked well. Matthew muses now that his skills in pastoral counseling aided his banking career. Matthew and Anne purchased a home of their own (still within a reasonable commute of the church) and had a second child. And the church grew stronger. It was not much later that he and church leaders realized the church was ready to have a fully funded minister. "We actually did a visioning thing—my first attempt at strategic planning," he said. Anne and he both prayerfully thought about the shift to him being a fully funded minister. They concluded that it was a great thing, and a right thing, for the church—and that Matthew wasn't the person to do it. They said goodbye to the people of that wonderful church, and Matthew turned his energies to being branch manager (he had been promoted), husband, and father.

Yet, not long after that, the regional minister called him and asked him if he would help a congregation as an interim minister. He said 'yes,' as long as he could keep his banking job. Soon

Matthew was realizing that his work in the banking world gave him valuable skills that were helpful to congregations, especially when they had "bad math problems." In the following thirty years, Matthew's banking career expanded and he served six other congregations, sometimes as an interim and other times as a long-term pastor (he served one for nineteen years). In addition to preaching and giving pastoral care to people, he helped these congregations look at their financial matters carefully and engage in strategic planning. In his many years of ministry, he also used his financial knowledge and skills by serving on the budgeting, administration, and transformation committees and other leadership roles in the D.C. region. In addition, he served on several boards at the general church level within the Disciples of Christ.

The story of Matthew's experience provides a glimpse of how bivocational ministry can strengthen God's church when given support. Such ministry enables individual ministers to use their gifts more fully, allows congregations to benefit from those gifts more fully, and enriches the wider church. In Matthew's case, "ministry thrived with support" as he responded to the help offered him in ways that also expanded his service to God and the church.

Clearly, congregations with bivocational pastors have an essential role in the mixed ecology of the twenty-first-century ministry landscape. Though they have been overshadowed at times by large churches and those with fully funded pastors, these churches are engaged in vital ministry, along rural highways, on Main Street in towns, nestled in established congregations in urban areas, and in rental space in office complexes and strip malls. The ministry of these congregations and their pastors furthers the gospel in diverse communities as part of the wider mission of the church in the world.

FOR REFLECTION AND DISCUSSION

1. What congregations in your community have lead pastors who are bivocational ministers? What about ministry staff who also work outside the church? What do you know about their other employment and how it connects with their ministry in the congregation?

2. What evidence have you seen or heard that supports the term "full-time bias"?

3. Looking at Rev. Matthew's story, name some of the support and encouragement that led him to "become bivocational." How could this kind of support and encouragement be more present in your context?

CHAPTER 2

Listening to Those Involved

"People need to hear from those of us doing the work," insisted one bivocational minister. Others agree. Hearing from people "doing the work" helps others understand what it's like, why it matters, and what might be done to make it better. This chapter features stories of two bivocational ministers and includes common observations made by lay leaders and ministers about disadvantages as well as advantages they experience.

For more than a dozen years, Pastor Tom has led Roadside Christian Church, a rural, predominantly white church in Kentucky. Prior to serving Roadside Christian Church, for most of his life Tom lived and worked in a town close to the church. He was a respected educator and elected official, as well as an active lay leader in another Disciples of Christ church. In 2009 Tom received a phone call from a leader of Roadside, who asked if he would consider being their minister. The call surprised him. He told me, "I immediately asked them why they had called me; I had no training." He listened carefully and began to wonder. Was this what God wanted him to do? What about the education that most ministers had? He knew Roadside had previously been led by seminary-trained ministers; he wondered how he would compare to them. After praying and speaking with trusted friends and his minister, he responded:

> I decided [to respond affirmatively] because I had always tried to determine how I was supposed to be serving. So I kept asking God, "Is this what you want me to do?" Finally, I realized I was asking the wrong question. I've always asked about serving, and now I see this is how God wants

me to serve. It was like, all of a sudden: "Here is your chance; now go do it." I accepted their call.

After being installed as pastor, he sought out continuing education opportunities to fulfill requirements for commissioning. He took seasonal and online classes scheduled around his other commitments. He also wanted to develop skills and expand knowledge to be a better minister: "One of the things the search committee stressed ... was that they were looking for a spiritual leader. That has stuck with me. I try to provide that as best as I can. ... I hope that I can fulfill their needs as a spiritual leader," he said. After being commissioned, Tom took more continuing education courses and joined other ministers in reading groups and monthly district minister meetings.

Reflecting on his preparation to become a commissioned minister, he said that he and others in the classes learned a great deal from the instructors and even more from each other. Other students were, like him, already serving as pastors (and many of them were bivocational). They would share and reflect with each other about how they were fulfilling the responsibilities of ministry. His commitment to lifelong learning has helped him to grow in his faith and strengthen his gifts for ministry as he continues in bivocational ministry at Roadside Christian Church.

The same year Tom became a pastor near where he lived, Philip traveled from Ghana to the U.S. with hopes of "learn[ing] and lead[ing] in the church." He attended seminary in the U.S. and explored ministry opportunities while also working along with his wife to support their family of five. He worked a variety of jobs—making retail deliveries, driving for Uber, and cleaning houses with his wife. This additional income helped Philip and his wife support their family. By 2023 he had earned his M.Div. degree, been ordained with the Disciples of Christ, completed Clinical Pastoral Education training, and started a new church.

During these years, his family faced significant financial challenges. He and his wife had to work long hours, which meant they had less time to spend together as a family. For many years with the new church Philip pastored without pay to enable the church to get on its feet. He said the church now provides some funds for housing and helps him with retirement through contributions to the Pension Fund of the Christian Church.

Before coming to the U.S., Philip had been a leader in churches in Ghana while also teaching school. He compared his work in the U.S. to that of missionaries. He worked by engaging with the people around him in the U.S. where he lived and worked. He also went to churches in the area with people from African countries and participated in some of them. He encountered many cultural and theological differences. After some time, he began leading a Friday night Bible study, whose participants eventually felt called to establish their own church.

As he considered starting a new church, Philip met with the Disciples of Christ regional minister. Their conversations led to the establishment of a pan-African congregation, Mission Street Christian Church (DOC), now over eight years old. Its mission and membership cross boundaries of culture and language. Its members are from Ghana, Republic of the Congo, Liberia, Nigeria, Senegal, and Sierra Leone. The church rents space in a business complex from a landlord who reduced the rent to help the church remain there. The church began to develop several types of support programs for people, including transportation and food. Philip said the best part of their church is Sunday worship in two languages (English and French with an interpreter) with joyful singing and dancing. Philip and the other leaders in the church meet on Saturday evenings to plan and prepare for the Sunday worship. Philip usually takes the remainder of Saturday as his day of rest since he works outside of the church the remainder of the week. He said that working so much has been a challenge but that it has allowed the church to pursue its special mission.

OBSERVATIONS OF CONGREGATIONS AND MINISTERS

Scheduling Is a Challenge

Figuring out "what's happening when" is tough when ministers are balancing responsibilities and tasks in more than one workplace. In fact, it's challenging for pastors whether their other jobs are part time or full time. But the challenges look different based on "what," "when," and "how much" ministers are trying to include in their schedules. What does their employment outside the church require? Does their work require a significant commute? Is remote work an option? How flexible are their work schedules? Are there time conflicts in their responsibilities at church and their other employment? Are people in their other workplaces (especially their bosses) supportive of their role with the church? Likewise, how supportive are people in the church of their other work?

One minister remarked on how the church took his work schedule into account when arranging committee meetings: "They schedule things primarily on Wednesdays or Sundays because those are the days I'm there." When there are conflicts, adjustments need to be made. One of the bivocational ministers also teaching high school takes it all in stride: "When I have a mandatory school meeting [that conflicts with] a mandatory church meeting ... I pick the one I would rather be at. You get to a point where you are overbooked; you just have to pick one. You cannot do both."

Technology can help address this challenge. One minister said, "The fact that my other job is remote means I can do it anywhere, as long as I have internet or a phone." Smartphones, online calendars, video-conferencing platforms such as Zoom, as well as other apps and programs that sync with others, certainly help. However, technology can create obstacles for effective ministry. For example, it has the capacity to distract. It's difficult for pastors (or any person) to pay attention and focus on intended work when interrupted by notifications of text messages and other information. In addition, there can be a steep learning curve to be able to use new technology. Some bivocational pastors testified to being overwhelmed with what was required to get everything in place for broadcasting or using video conferencing for their congregations during the COVID-19 pandemic. Technology can be time-consuming and expensive to fund and understand, particularly given its rapid changes and updates. Finding the appropriate technological tools is important, especially when smaller budgets, unreliable internet connections, and lack of technological expertise allow little wiggle room.

Reflecting on the challenges that a tight schedule presented over the years, one minister admitted he had been forced to work on his skills in this area: "I think being bivocational has taught me how to schedule and be a better steward of my time." All ministers testified that there are times that require a delicate balancing act, such as certain seasons of the church year or when they are needed for funerals.

One result of complicated scheduling is that many bivocational ministers have few opportunities to gather with others, especially with other bivocational ministers, as that would require them to take off time from work, perhaps without pay, or to use vacation time. The same is true for professional meetings related to their other jobs; attending such meetings requires them to take time off from church work. Similar challenges emerge when scheduling family vacations or trips, planning for continuing education, and creating opportunities for Sabbath rest.

Overload Is a Real Possibility for the Pastor

Bivocational ministers are often tempted to try to do more than they can realistically accomplish. Those inside and outside the church, their friends and family members, and they themselves place (unrealistic) expectations on them. For example, one bivocational minister named Len worked forty hours a week at another job while also serving a congregation with an aging membership and significant financial struggles. After efforts to address financial shortfalls and to transform their ministry, the church sold its building. Subsequently they were nesting in a building that belonged to another church when their leaders recognized the time might be near for them to close—a decision made all the more difficult because many of the congregation's older members had been part of the church their entire lives.

Yet for Len, exhaustion was the biggest challenge:

Commuting is not a challenge. Scheduling is not a challenge; people are very accommodating. Financial challenges are not a problem. ... The biggest thing as it impacts me is [that] I find myself, over a long haul, being mentally exhausted at times ... and the mental exhaustion leads to spiritual exhaustion.

Part of Len's exhaustion was the genuine love and care he had for the members. He said:

> I worry for our older members that if we are unable to make it, where will they go? Will they find a place to call home? ... They were heartbroken when we had to leave our old building. I think they will be heartbroken if we have to close. That will break my heart. I think I worry about them as individuals more than I worry about the collective congregation.

His concerns and cares were real, and his schedule hardly ever gave him a break to rest or to manage the emotions he was experiencing. He recognized the toll it was taking on his life.

Many bivocational ministers are similarly concerned about their work-life balance. For example, they have said: "I need to ... guard time for rest and Sabbath, ... gain comfort in saying 'no,' ... better recognize my limits, and improve my boundaries." Some are working under unrealistic expectations in their churches, where they hear comparisons with larger churches that have one or more ministers paid to work full time in the church. Some feel guilty or apologetic about what they do not have time to accomplish in their church.

Like other ministers, those who are bivocational can end up making themselves "over-available" to serve and help others. Minister and professor of pastoral ministry Kirk Byron Jones notes that Christian ministers and other caregivers can suffer from an "unbalanced theology of sacrifice," and cautions that "in Christianity, self-care is ignored to the detriment of clergy and their families."[14]

Some Ministry Doesn't Get Done

While many lay leaders say they're satisfied with the way ministry is accomplished, others say some facets of ministry don't get enough attention in their churches because their minister is bivocational. One said: "Following up on visitors, I think that is a

---

[14] Kirk Byron Jones, *Rest in the Storm: Self-Care Strategies for Clergy and Other Caregivers*, 20th anniversary ed. (Valley Forge, PA: Judson Press, 2021), 15–16.

concern. We should be doing more ... to follow up on some of that. That concerns me a little bit." A lay leader in another church sees youth ministry as an area that is left out and wishes the minister could do more. Observations regarding gaps in ministry differ. Some observers imagine what their ministers would do if they had more time, some complain about their minister's priorities, and others say the gaps need to be addressed by laypeople.

Some of what "gets left out" may be easily handled. One pair of lay leaders discussed what happened when their current bivocational minister replaced one who had lived in the parsonage:

> When the minister was living in the parsonage, if something needed to be done at church ... or UPS was delivering a package, they could usually go to the house, and somebody was there. ... Now it's just that somebody needs to be there. ... If we want to set something up, we just plan on being there ourselves. From a leadership standpoint, in the church itself, probably not much was affected.

They agreed that, while that shift was inconvenient, it worked out once they noticed which tasks needed to be done by someone other than the minister.

Visiting and providing pastoral care to people are mentioned often as areas of ministry needing more attention. Some lay leaders say they know of members concerned that the minister did not visit members enough. Others disagree and think visitation is a form of ministry that those in the congregation could engage in more. In one interview a lay leader said: "I don't think the thing about visitation is a shortcoming on [the minister's] part as much as it is a shortcoming on the congregation's part for not helping more with that. ... I feel that if there is anybody that thinks there is not enough visitation being done, they need to step up and do it." Some churches have informal networks of members who do home visits. Some have well-developed teams of members who visit others who are sick, confined to their homes, or living in nursing homes. Others assign responsibility for visitation to elders and deacons. In many cases, ministers are expected to call on those in the hospital, having surgery, or other prioritized needs.

Regardless of these differences, many church members understand that ministry is not the sole responsibility of the minister. They recognize the church cannot and indeed should not rely on the minister to get everything done.

Strong Lay Leadership is Key, AND...

Bivocational ministers praise people in their churches for the many ways they enrich the church's ministry and collaborate with them. One said, "This is the most self-sufficient congregation I have ever experienced." This pastor said the leaders took responsibility for scheduling meetings, nominating and electing leaders, coordinating mission projects, and keeping people in touch with each other. The leaders kept the pastor informed, yet they did the planning themselves. Such increased involvement tends to strengthen the lay leaders' ownership of the church's ministry. They come to see themselves as the pastor's partners in ministry.

Unfortunately, such collaborative leadership is not always present. Some ministers note a lack of lay leadership or see unhealthy power dynamics. Some congregations have a small group of leaders who dominate the leadership. It's not always clear why this happens. Are some in the church holding back because they don't recognize their own gifts or capacity to lead? Are some staying in leadership because they can't see others have the gifts or capacity to lead? Or are some leaders actively or passively discouraging others from taking part? These difficulties may be deeply rooted (for individuals, families, and congregations) and can be further complicated when church membership primarily consists of a few extended families.

It is a common misconception that strong pastoral leadership results in weak lay leadership, and vice versa. In reality, when pastors and lay leaders work together in supportive collaboration, they strengthen one another. Learning how to manage this "both/and" ministry relationship is key to strengthening bivocational ministry.

Lay leaders agree that increased participation happens when the church has a bivocational pastor. The constraints on the minister's time create openings for others to take on ministry roles. These openings also help church members to emerge as leaders and to deepen their sense of ministry as a shared vocation rather than as the sole responsibility of a pastor. Although some congregations have greater lay participation than others, increased lay participation is a central and positive impact of bivocational ministry. Many congregations with a tradition of bivocational ministry have well-developed lay participation. A lay leader in such a congregation describes this:

> We are a small church, but very committed members, dedicated members, who look out for each other. Most ... everybody in the church is involved in some form or fashion in supporting the church. And I don't just mean financially, I mean serving on committees and things like that. So we're small, but we're committed and faithful.

One minister mentioned his own experience as a lay leader: "I try to get them involved. We have some wonderful lay people who are very capable. ... Coming from a lay leadership background myself, I certainly try to encourage and promote it in the church."

It Makes Ministry Better

For many bivocational ministers, being employed outside the church strengthens their ministry. A common observation is that it allows a cross-pollination of skills and knowledge. One commissioned minister, also working in a family business, said his financial training at work was indispensable to his ministry. Ministers who work in business, accounting, or banking use skills developed at work to help churches with financial statements, budgeting, and financial planning. Ministers working in government agencies or as nonprofit leaders have valuable experience managing programs and services and working with diverse groups of people. A minister who also teaches college said, "Being a teacher helps me be a better minister, helps me be a better communicator."

Ministers report that their employment outside the church helps them to understand the experiences of people in their congregations. One veteran bivocational minister pointed out, "I am more understanding of the perils people have ... when there is a potential of someone losing a job or when they change insurance at work." Another bivocational minister agreed:

> The thing is ... when something happens upstream [in the company where they're employed], your life is dramatically affected. ... "Oh, we got bought out; will I still have a job?" Those kinds of things are now part of my life. When the VP says, "You have to do this on this day," that is now part of my reality. I think it has helped me better understand the experience of other people.

By participating in the world of everyday work, these ministers expand their awareness of challenges people face in daily life as well as opportunities to live faithfully in daily life. The majority of their time is not confined within the boundaries of the congregation, which is already friendly to "tried and true ways" of doing ministry. Instead, they are working in an environment where receptivity to Christian faith is "cool, sometimes cold."[15] By participating in the everyday, these ministers find ways to strengthen, in both word and deed, the ministry of the church in the world.

For some pastors, their work outside the church helps them respond more nimbly and richly to church-related issues. Work responsibilities that are different from those at church enable them to gain a different and perhaps more objective perspective to understand what's happening at the church. One minister explained how the thirty-minute drive home from church provides time for him to process things: "If there is an issue at the church, I process mentally on the commute. So, when I get home, I am not tied up in knots about something that is going on at church."

For others, the welcome relief of additional income in a bivocational arrangement can reduce stress and help make ministry better. One pastor testified to experiencing financial stress before finding a second part-time position: "I can't put into words the kind of financial stress we've been under since before the pandemic." After finding a second job, another minister said, "I now can swipe my debit card and I do not have to go through

---

[15] William Diehl, *Ministry in Daily Life: A Practical Guide for Congregations* (New York: Alban Institute, 1996), 11.

this mental spiral of shame wondering, 'Is this thing going to be declined?'"

Such financial relief might not sound like something that makes someone a better minister. Yet the income from the church for some ministers falls well below what is needed to meet normal living standards. Some carry burdensome debt, often including student loans. According to authority on well-being and work Matt Bloom's *Flourishing in Ministry* research, financial concerns can have a significant and negative impact on ministers' well-being. Having insufficient income to support their needs and those of their household is often unspoken, yet the concerns impact their work and life and can cause their pastoral effectiveness to be diminished.[16] Having both the income from the church and employment outside the church can relieve these stressors and contribute to ministers' well-being, improving the ways they serve the church.

WHAT'S NEXT?

For ministers and lay leaders alike, the future is uncertain. Some are wondering, "What's next for us?" During the COVID-19 pandemic, some churches were able to introduce livestreamed services. Some wondered whether their members would return to in-person worship. Others, who have recovered well enough and have a strong sense of their role in God's mission, may be able to embrace the future with a more adventuresome spirit. Pastor Philip said Mission Street Christian Church's next steps are to "let go of some programs damaged by COVID-19 and focus on our worship; it is our strength." Pastor Tom spoke with enthusiasm about a missional partnership he is establishing along with ministers of four smaller churches within fifteen miles of Roadside Christian Church. In 2023 their ecumenical ministerial association studied the book *Together Is Better: How Small Membership Churches Fulfill God's Missional Call through Partnerships.*[17] Afterward, these ministers from four different denominations decided to work

[16] Matt Bloom, *Flourishing in Ministry: How to Cultivate Clergy Well-being* (Lanham, MD: Rowman and Littlefield, 2019), 11.

[17] Lisa Culpepper, *Together Is Better: How Small Membership Churches Fulfill God's Missional Call through Partnerships* (self-pub., 2021).

collaboratively to transform the way they enact God's mission and help people in their community.

No matter what a church is facing, laity and ministers can trust God to work in all things for good (Rom. 8:28). Instead of being pessimistic or optimistic about the future, they can be hopeful. One pastor expressed a hopeful attitude about the future like this:

> We have talked about this in meetings: we are in decline. There is no question; we can look at the numbers, year over year, and know that it is a slow, steady decline. I worry about how many generations we are from extinction. ... I do not know if that is because of bivocational ministry, I think it is just in general for this church. ... One thing we do have is financial resources and generous stewards. This is where I am focusing, at the moment, to say, "OK, we are not going to worry about numbers, we are just going to do the ministry we are called to do, for as long as we are able to do it." If that yields some participation, then great. ... We can still do some great ministry here.

In this chapter we have looked at opportunities and challenges that bivocational ministers and their congregations experience. The next three chapters will include specific help to navigate those challenges and take advantage of those opportunities to make a difference with faithful ministry.

FOR REFLECTION AND DISCUSSION

1. What do you notice about Tom and Philip's stories? What is similar and different about their experiences? What is significant about those similarities and differences?

2. In the observations made by congregations and ministers in this chapter, what surprises you and/or resonates with your experience?

3. What's next for you or your congregation as you work to serve God's mission where you are located?

CHAPTER 3

Wisdom for Congregations

"I hope they know how to make it workable!" A Lexington Theological Seminary student who is a bivocational minister left this comment in a 2018 survey about what these students hope their congregations know about bivocational ministry. Some congregations *do* know how to make such ministry workable. They have learned to cultivate a fertile environment for bivocational ministry. These congregations have found that it's in everyone's best interest to be a place where ministers and congregations can thrive together. Many of the lessons they've learned come from decades of experience with pastors who had other jobs.

Pastor Bill was blessed to find such a congregation in Township Christian Church when he became bivocational there for the first time. Township, a predominantly white church, is located in a large, well-maintained building on the main street of a small town a forty-minute commute from where Bill lived and worked. Through the years, several different ministers who also had other jobs have led Township. One of its most beloved former pastors served the church for more than twenty-five years while teaching school and serving as an elected official in town.

Bill was working a full-time "corporate job" when a regional minister encouraged him to consider serving Township while still working his job. Bill had been out of ministry for a few years, previously serving as a lead minister of a large congregation until he burned out from church conflict and work overload. Regarding that decision, he wished things had been different, but he was still relieved to have left behind the sense he was a walking target in the congregation he had led.

Not long into his time with Township, Bill realized this ministry experience would be different. He was delighted to find knowledgeable and caring lay leaders who took responsibility for many tasks that had been expected of him in his previous situation. Lay leaders willingly partnered with him in pastoral care, both visiting and praying with people. They didn't depend on him to supply the ideas and plans for the church's mission and ministry within the surrounding community. He said, "They take care of each other really well ... and they take care of the church." Bill appreciated how they knew what needed to be done throughout the year, including decorating the sanctuary, taking care of the church property, and nominating and electing new elders and deacons. They expected him to lead worship and gave him freedom to preach "with a prophetic tone" when called to do so. Not only did Township know "how to make it work," but they became a place of healing where Bill rediscovered his sense of call to congregational ministry.

Pastor Arvell likewise serves a congregation that knows how to make bivocational ministry work. He is the lead pastor of Valleyview Christian Church, a historically Black congregation in a small town in the eastern U.S. He had this to say about bivocational ministry and how it works with his congregation:

> It is a wonderful balance if you have a congregation that will work with you. ... I live about an hour and fifteen minutes, driveway to driveway, but when they call me during the week, it's to ask, "Pastor, can you pray for me? I have this going on." There's no underlying, "We want you to drive here when you get off work at five thirty and get here at seven and drive back." They have been wonderful to me. Wonderful.

Arvell is not Valleyview's first bivocational pastor. He attributes much of what works well in the congregation to its previous bivocational pastor, who served there for sixteen years, also with a significant commute. "They became used to having a pastor not right next door, not ten minutes away," he said. "I'm very thankful that on Sunday morning at nine thirty, when I pull up, they are not looking at me saying, 'You're the one who does the stuff.' They see themselves, I think, as disciples."

Arvell's call to ministry came after he had finished college and after he had worked for several years in "corporate America." He said that he had "wanted to wear a suit and tie five days a week." Yet he found that life unsatisfactory: "There was dissatisfaction about what I thought would make me happy. The more I found myself involved in church work, the more God was speaking to me very softly." He transitioned to working for nonprofit organizations and then also pastoring. Before coming to Valleyview in 2018, he served as a minister of pastoral care alongside a lead pastor who had shown him how bivocational ministry could bring joy and balance in a pastor's life.

Arvell and the congregation have developed a trusting relationship. He is present at the church each Sunday as well as on one or two Saturdays each month to visit with church members. He said it is significant when people trust their pastor. "Someone was going through a crisis," he said, "and they wanted to get me alone in a corner to say, 'Pastor, I need you to intercede to God for my son, my kidney, my diabetes, my surgery next Wednesday. And I trust that you have a relationship with God.' ... It is humbling when people trust you."

Ministers like Bill and Arvell benefit from leading congregations with years of experience with bivocational ministry. Clearly, congregations learn from their experience! Fortunately, congregations without that same "firsthand" experience can take steps toward developing a shared ministry with a bivocational minister. One of the most hopeful components of the model of bivocational ministry is the way it reopens conversations about the shape of congregational leadership.

WORDS OF WISDOM

Examine Your Expectations of Your Minister

Many bivocational ministers report they have twenty to twenty-five hours per week for focused church-related work. Depending on the nature of their other employment, they also may have limits on both "how much" and "when" they have time for ministry with the church. For instance, ministers who also work as full-time teachers have different schedules and responsibilities than do those who also work part time in a nonprofit or those who make their living by balancing several hourly wage jobs. When congregations understand their ministers' limitations, they adapt their expectations of both their ministers and themselves to make it work.

When congregations share a clear sense of their expectations, ministers are better able to discern how their lives fit with a congregation's needs. This is very helpful when congregations are in the process of looking for a new minister. Reviewing those expectations is likewise useful when ministers are already serving a congregation. Such examinations enable members and ministers to reflect on priorities so that they accomplish what is most important for their ministry together.

Writer and church leader Mark Edington proposes a simple way to begin examining the expectations that congregations have of their ministers. When he became the new pastor of a small congregation while also working as a publisher, he used two questions as powerful tools to help the congregation move away from a model of a pastor-centered ministry: "What do you expect the pastor to do?" and "How necessary is it for the pastor to do that?" These questions led to a bigger discussion as the pastor and congregation together explored how to develop a more group-centered culture in the congregation where they were in the ministry "together."[18]

While potentially helpful for all congregations, questions like these are especially important for those with bivocational ministers. Unfortunately, many congregations have not reflected fully on expectations of ministers they have inherited from the past. Here's how one retired bivocational minister explained the dilemma:

> For me, bivocational ministry meant serving in a church that could not afford to pay a minister a full-time compensation package, which could include one, some, or all these benefits: a living wage or salary, insurance, utilities, pension, education allowance, travel, etc. I always had another means of employment that made it possible

---

[18] Mark Edington, *Bivocational*, 52–53.

for me to serve a small church. Although I received a part-time package, the churches I served expected me to be a full-time minister. Too often the church leadership was weak or did not live up to expectations as church leaders. The churches also wanted me to either live in the community where the church was located or as close as possible.

Congregations may begin to envision what ministry looks like in their own context with a bivocational minister with these two questions. Adding a third question—"Who else in our congregation has the gifts to do that?"—might also be helpful. Exploring "who" is engaged in "what" ministry and "why" can be a creative process. The process can spark members to recognize their own call and capacity to participate in ministry, something to which all Christians are called through their baptism. In this process, names of those already present in the congregation may emerge as having gifts for ministry that have not been fully used. They may well become partners in a shared ministry alongside the minister. (See Appendix A for a worksheet about ministry expectations that could be helpful in this process.)

Once expectations have been clarified, it is good to "put them in writing." This advice comes from an experienced bivocational minister. He explained how, after serving in several bivocational settings, he learned the benefit of clarifying expectations with a congregation then recording them in a written ministry agreement. The written document helped everyone in the church know how much he would be available. If a congregation does adopt this practice, it is best done in collaboration with a minister, allowing ministers to express their understanding of their gifts and priorities for ministry as well as challenges related to their other employment. Agreements for bivocational ministry work well when they take into account a minister's unique situation, including other employment, as well as a congregation's needs, resources, and ministry priorities.

Operate from a Perspective of Sufficiency

Congregations that are most successful with bivocational ministry have learned to look at what they "have" more than worrying about what they "don't have." Even when congregations are concerned about decline, looking at the resources they have as "sufficient" is an important step in making a difference in ministry where they are located. One of the keys for congregations operating from a perspective of sufficiency is moving away from comparing themselves to others and, instead, accepting themselves as "enough." According to fundraiser and philanthropist Lynne Twist, "sufficiency" is when "we engage in life from a sense of our own wholeness rather than a desperate longing to be complete. We feel naturally called to share the resources that flow through our lives—our time, our money, our wisdom, our energy, at whatever level those resources flow—to serve our highest commitments."[19]

Many congregations have remarkable assets they have been overlooking, and it can feel like a revelation when they shift to a perspective of sufficiency. Once they focus on what they have, they begin to uncover its value for meaningful ministry. For instance, a church with a large building with lots of empty space shifts to become a place where nonprofits and a new church find a welcome home. A church with numerous members who cannot leave home invites them to become intercessors for others in the church and community. A church with lots of retired members engages their combined talents to develop an after-school cooking club for neighborhood elementary school children. When churches recognize that whatever they have has been provided by God, they discover energy and enthusiasm to discern how to use it to serve God.

A small storefront church with a bivocational pastor found a "small and significant" strategy that was just what they needed one Advent season. They started off lamenting how little they were compared to the big church whose driveway wound up the hill behind their building. Each Sunday they saw the steady flow of cars driving up to the big church. They remembered that the church hosted a cantata before Christmas each year and imagined the parade of cars driving past them for that big pageant.

---

[19] Lynne Twist, *The Soul of Money: Transforming Your Relationship with Money and Life* (New York: W.W. Norton and Co., 2017), 75.

Feeling down, someone lamented, "They don't even know we are here." Then someone else commented, "That's how it was back then, too; people walked right past the place where Jesus was born." From that comment, an idea took root: they would create their own nativity scene as an answer to the question, "Where would Jesus be born in our town today?"

They cleared space around the back door of their building and foraged for material around town to set up a makeshift stable with a manger. One person found a barrel that had been used to burn trash, and others found old, discarded wood. As the work progressed, another member proposed they create life-size silhouettes of church members. He asked everyone to stay after church one Sunday, set up a way to cast their shadows on the wall, then traced the shadows and used them to make plywood figures, which he painted black. The silhouettes were stationed (and secured with wires) around the scene.

By the beginning of Advent they were ready to begin worship outside each week (wearing their coats), with the Call to Worship at the nativity scene. They then processed through the back door and the church storage room into their usual worship space. The whole project brought them a sense of joy and affirmed their role in their community. Reflecting on how many people in his time had overlooked the power of Jesus' birth empowered them to continue ministry in his name, despite being overlooked themselves.

Many lay leaders in congregations with bivocational ministers communicate a sense of sufficiency when they speak enthusiastically of what they do in their communities—as individuals and as congregations. Some say, "It's not that much," but they also say, "We give what we have." They list things like helping neighbors in times of crisis, serving as volunteer firefighters, collecting for local food banks and community assistance programs, advocating for justice reform, delivering meals, working on fundraisers for local nonprofits, serving as school crossing guards, helping with community gardens, donating supplies to local schools, helping with voter registration, serving as poll workers, cleaning riverways, and picking up trash in neighborhoods. They write checks, too, providing financial support for community projects and missions around the world through individual contributions and special offerings. In their generosity with what they have, they make a difference.

Take the Pulse of the Church Body's Health

"We always make sure there's hugging on Sundays," smiled one congregational leader. "We know most of our older members live alone; they need some hugs." This comment reflects one of the many ways belonging to a congregation offers an alternative to the loneliness, division, and alienation many people experience in daily life. Church members know about this; they frequently describe their congregations as "friendly" and "loving" and as places where "everyone is welcome." Many people, especially those in congregations where members frequently experience marginalization, see their congregation as offering hope and love in a world that does not exhibit much care for them. If asked what it means to belong to "the church" or "the body of Christ" (an image the apostle Paul frequently used for the church), many would not think first of being on an official membership list. Instead, they would think of being part of a Christian community where they know and are known by others.

How is this participation or membership managed? Congregations that are led by bivocational ministers do not rely on the ministers to lead these efforts. With the responsibilities of their other employment, such ministers have limits that interfere with the work required in creating and sustaining a culture of "belonging" in a congregation. Many of these congregations have a perfectly well-developed capacity to help people sense that they belong. They create opportunities for people to participate, and they host events that gather people together so they can hold conversations, catch up on news, and "care for each other." Often the gatherings involve food, such as Sunday potluck meals after worship, seasonal cookouts, and fish fries. One congregation with many hunters holds "wild game dinners" and opens modern gun deer season each fall with a "blessing of the hunt." Regarding one congregation's numerous and various meals, a church member said, "It's just part of the culture—this hospitality around tables and feeding folks." Other traditions in congregations that give people opportunities to deepen their relationships with each other include providing time for testimony and praying for people during worship, hosting groups that meet for prayer and studies, singalongs, and game nights. Individuals also take it from there, beyond gatherings, groups, or traditions hosted by congregations, as they hold conversations, share ideas and resources, visit and care for each other, and collaborate in the work of ministry, in and outside their congregations.

Yet these congregations, like others, also include people who feel they don't fully belong. It may be unclear why they feel that way. Have they been judged or pushed aside? Do they have unresolved conflict with others in the church? Are they experiencing unrecognized suffering of some kind? For various reasons, they linger on the margins. This is a disturbing scenario for congregations as communities with God's love for all people through Jesus Christ at their very heart. While it may appear that people belong to a particular congregation because they are "alike" in some way—such as by age, ethnicity/race, socioeconomic status, or being part of the same extended family—they are actually and more essentially bound together by the love of Jesus Christ. The relationships people have "in Christ" actually surpass, or transform, all the other similarities and relationships. The special bond of "being in Christ" is part of a congregation's very heart. Congregations need to do what they can to strengthen and extend love and care to suffuse those on the margins, too.

Sometimes congregations need to analyze what they do and discern whether they are drawing people together and "building up the body of Christ" (Eph. 4:12) or contributing to barriers that keep people apart. The pan-African congregation led by Pastor Philip (his story appeared in chapter 2), Mission Street Christian Church, reflected on the language it uses in worship. The congregation includes both English- and French-language speakers. Since their founding, they have all worshipped together in the English language with French translation. However, leaders realized that perhaps this practice benefitted the English speakers more than the French speakers. It had created a power barrier in their relationship that needed to be re-aligned. They were discussing changes. What if they held worship entirely in French with English translation? Or what about hosting two different worship services so that the French-speaking members no longer had "second-class" status?

The leaders of Mission Street were fully aware they were a multicultural community. They spent time reflecting on what it meant for the congregation to have two languages in worship but with one always translated from the other. They realized that what was happening in their combined-language worship, although meant to draw people together, was actually contributing to barriers between people. They did what ministry consultant Eric Law states is "critical" for multicultural congregations if they are "to live out the fullness of the Gospel": a power analysis.[20] Then, following that analysis, the leaders were "called to be 'Robin Hoods' of power—to take power from the powerful and give it to the powerless."[21] They did it as an act of humble service hoping to draw the people together.

Other congregations—those which perceive themselves as more "homogenous"—may also benefit from such a power analysis. Every congregation includes inequities of power—leaders, insiders, and others who have power versus those who have less.

Leaders in congregations may find it helpful to follow Eric Law's own example when considering the kinds of power people have in their congregations. About his own power in a community where he is respected as a leader, he said: "I use my power very carefully. I become very humble and try to find ways to empower others."[22] Being humble and thinking of the needs of others are good steps for leaders to take as they contemplate how well their congregation is drawing people together. Asking questions and reflecting about relationships and communal practices in congregations may be helpful. The following questions are worth considering:

- How are people supported and prayed for in the congregation? What human experiences or suffering

---

[20] Eric Law, *The Wolf Shall Dwell with the Lamb: A Spirituality for Leadership in a Multicultural Community* (St. Louis, MO: Chalice Press, 1993), 57.

[21] Law, *The Wolf*, 74.

[22] Law, *The Wolf*, 75.

are typically included in—and left out of—those prayers?

- How are people of all ages and their households nurtured to deepen their relationship with God and expand the ways they interpret scripture?

- What helps people in the congregation deepen their relationships with one another?

- What is done in the congregation to help people expand their circles of relationships to include those whom they do not already know well?

- What explicit support is provided to welcome newcomers to worship services and help them—and everyone else—know "what to do" during worship?

- What is done to address human conflict and division so people identify their need for reconciliation?

- What is done to affirm, equip, and support people for ministry inside the congregation as well as in the wider community?

Community and communication are closely related. A congregation's communication practices matter—the way in which individuals talk to each other, about each other, and about the ministry they do together. Communication practices can draw people together or contribute to barriers. For instance, congregations help individuals come to know each other better when they enable them to address each other by name and connect with each other for further conversation. When congregations can provide shared contact lists or church directories that include names and contact information, as well as other things of interest, they help draw people together. Likewise, keeping everyone "in the loop" about congregational care and ministry activities also matters. It's helpful when everyone in the congregation, including newcomers, knows "the 5 W's"—Who? What? When? Where? Why?—of events or ministry activities. Another big challenge for congregations in the twenty-first century is determining "which way" to communicate with the myriad of technological tools now available. When congregations determine which tools work best for them and develop sound habits using them, technology can support effective communication in the church community.

A congregation's practices related to the way individuals talk to each other and about each other also have the potential to draw people together or contribute to barriers for their sense of belonging to the ministry of Jesus Christ. For instance, imagine a congregation that has heretofore seen itself in the role of a "landlord" instead of adopting the role of the "innkeeper" in the parable of the good Samaritan (Lk. 10:25–37) when renting out space in their church building to nonprofit organizations. I imagine that letting go of the identity of "landlord" and taking on that of the "innkeeper" would help draw people into a stronger sense of ministry participation. Or what about church members who begin seeing the "dirty work" of their congregation (e.g., administrative work on committees or work groups) as a current-day form of "foot-washing" (Jn. 13:1–15)? I imagine this change might help them embrace committee work as humble service that people who follow Jesus do for each other. Language can help or hinder a sense of identity and mission.

The language individuals use to address each other in congregations also can help to draw people together or contribute to barriers. Within some congregations, such as historically African American congregations, it is customary for people to address each other as "Sister Juanita" or "Brother John," an explicit recognition of the relationships they have "in Christ." Likewise, many use titles such as "Elder Hill" or "Deacon Smith" as a sign of respect for a person's servant-leadership role in the congregation. This is not unlike decisions within congregations about what words to use when referring to human beings that reflect the full value of the diversity of humankind, made in God's image. Many congregations in all contexts continue to struggle with their approach to inclusive language for humankind, as well as language for God that is expansive and reflects the full range of how God is honored, addressed, and referred to in the Bible. These struggles reflect the powerful influence of cultural and political divisions in society at large. Congregations and individuals do well to consider how their use of language about people and about God draws people together or contributes to barriers in "belonging to each other through Jesus Christ."[23]

At the most basic level, relationships are the heart of a strong and healthy community. By working to strengthen the sense of belonging to each other in ways that mirror the love of Jesus Christ, congregations help people to deepen their care for each other, resist the loneliness rampant in the world today, and share in the work of Christ's ministry together.

Let the Gratitude Show

"Our church wouldn't be here if it weren't for our pastor." Comments like this one are frequent when church members talk about their bivocational pastors. They look at their ministers and how much they do alongside holding down that "other job," and they are grateful.

It's important for ministers to hear that gratitude. A simple "thank you" can frame the importance of daily gratitude and strengthen a sense of human connection. When ministers hear words like "thank you" and "we're grateful to you," it can be a breath of fresh air, especially if they don't receive much appreciation in their other employment. When expressions of thanks are "specific, personal, and genuine," they have an even greater impact.[24]

It may sound surprising, but public expressions of gratitude for ministers may encourage a wider sense of gratitude in the congregation. Public affirmations of a minister's leadership and ministry may kindle gratitude among those in the pews who are

---

[23] For a simple way to think about inclusive language for human beings the Linguistic Society of America has developed four rules as guidelines for inclusive language: it promotes the use of inclusive language that "acknowledges diversity, conveys respect to all people, is sensitive to difference, and promotes equal opportunities." For more, see https://www.lsadc.org/guidelines_for_inclusive_language. Expansive language for God aims to expand faithful ways for addressing God and referring to God to include the many words and images used for that purpose within the Bible. For some resources regarding expansive language with reference to God, see https://www.ucc.org/expansive-language-with-reference-to-god/.

[24] Bloom, *Flourishing in Ministry*, 108.

unaware or overlooking what the minister, as well as other leaders, does. An elder of one congregation told how he does this at the Lord's Supper in worship:

> Every Sunday that I'm at the communion table, and I may be leading communion, and when we finish communion, at the end of the service, I'll turn to the congregation and say words like: "Did we hear a great message today? Let's give our pastor a hand." You know, I'm making sure that he knows that we appreciate what he's doing. And not only him, but the musician, the ushers, and all, because they're doing a service. And so the congregation itself often tells him how happy they are that he's at our church. So he hears; he hears those words practically [every] Sunday.

When people hear words like this affirmation of the pastor, it helps refocus their attention on being thankful for the good things happening around them when they may be preoccupied with obstacles and challenges the congregation faces.

Many congregations have traditions of honoring their ministers at special times of the year. These are usually at times in congregational life when expressions of gratitude are in order, such as on the anniversary of a minister's call to the church, a minister's birthday, during Clergy Appreciation Month, as well as at the conclusion of their ministry or at their retirement. The pastor's anniversary is a key method of expressing appreciation for the minister in the African American context and also serves as an avenue for additional financial support. Some congregations go "all in" and plan special celebrations. Others make presentations, often simple, in connection with Sunday worship. All these practices can be good. Just like people in other contexts, ministers appreciate being remembered at special times.

A congregation also shows gratitude for bivocational ministers when actively engaging in practices that support their well-being in ministry. These practices include church members praying for ministers and their households, working collaboratively with ministers, respecting ministers' "time off" to allow for rest and replenishment, providing adequate compensation, and providing a healthy pastoral support group for encouragement and accountability. Such support also includes developing a congregational environment that deals proactively with destructive conflict and antagonism. When a minister faces times of conflict and experiences difficulties with individuals in congregations, it is painful. Bloom states the following about a consistent finding in his research on clergy well-being:

> One of the most potent and damaging factors for pastors' wellbeing is mistreatment by parishioners. Harsh criticism, disrespect, rejection, and ostracism are, unfortunately, common for a significant portion of pastors. ... Women and pastors of color are more often the target of mistreatment, and young pastors seem to be facing increasing incidents of harsh criticism and rejection.[25]

When mistreatment of ministers occurs and goes unaddressed, it takes a toll on them. Speaking up for ministers when they have been mistreated, interceding on their behalf, and/or providing support are affirmations of them as ministers and as human beings.

WE'RE IN THIS TOGETHER

This chapter began with the stories of Township and Valleyview Christian churches, where years of experience with bivocational ministry helped these congregations develop into communities where elders, deacons, and people in the pews find ways to work collaboratively with ministers. Even though Pastor Bill had no previous experience of being bivocational himself, the leaders of Township knew how to help him learn the ropes. At Valleyview, Pastor Arvell had more experience as a bivocational minister, and he expressed appreciation for the way people there knew how to work with him so he could be a good pastor from a distance. In both these congregations, the ministers and congregation members have a sense that "we're in this together."

The sense of community and shared ministry that helps bivocational ministry work well reflects the way the church comes together at the Lord's Supper. In Disciples congregations, elders

---

[25] Bloom, *Flourishing in Ministry*, 88.

say the prayers each week as people gather around the Lord's table. Amidst the discussions about bivocational ministry, one lay leader said this:

> We are able to set [our differences] aside to come to the table. This is a huge reason why I am in the Disciples church—this feature of being able to set aside our differences to come to God, to come to Christ's table.

The Lord's Supper is a weekly reminder that "we're in this together" with the people who make up the church and in the company of Jesus Christ. Pastors like Bill and Arvell have discovered that serving as bivocational ministers works better when everyone— ministers and laypeople alike—strengthens how they work (well) together, inside the circle of God's love. With this sense of collaboration, even congregations moving into bivocational ministry arrangements for the first time can develop the capacity for shared ministry; they can become places where "they know how to make it work."

FOR REFLECTION AND DISCUSSION

1. What do you notice about the stories of Bill and Arvell? What is similar and different about their experiences? What is significant about those similarities and differences?

2. What words of wisdom in this chapter surprise you and/or resonate with your experience?

3. What are some next steps that you or your congregation could take so that ministry is shared more fully?

CHAPTER 4

Wisdom for Ministers

If you ask bivocational ministers about their "typical" work week, they might laugh—for there's not much that could be called "typical." Even if their other employment has a steady schedule, church work varies depending on the time of the year. As we all know, the weeks before Christmas and Easter are busier than those right after Pentecost, which often coincides with the beginning of the summer break from school. However, most bivocational ministers never feel like they can put their feet up; they have full schedules all the time. Whether it's getting to the hospital to check on a church member, finishing a sermon, or meeting the next work deadline, their weeks are full. These ministers have plenty to accomplish. One minister commented on the cyclical way time moves through the various seasons of the year, admitting that sometimes it feels like "a hamster wheel." For many of these ministers, the key is pacing themselves as they move through that cycle of time. When they do that, they find this model of ministry more likely to be satisfying.

Pastor Terrence has been a bivocational minister for over forty years. For the past twenty-five he has been pastor of Streetside Christian Church, a historically Black church in the southeastern U.S., while also working as a high school history teacher and coach in a nearby town. When he first came to the Streetside congregation, it was embroiled in conflict. He stayed with them through difficulties and has witnessed the church stabilize and grow stronger. Now the church has grown to have an average of eighty people in worship on Sundays. They have made repairs to the church building and purchased property next door that had been neglected. Terrence is supported by a strong core of leaders who collaborate with him and share the ministry of pastoral care, prayer, and preaching. His leadership team also includes a group of young people who "help make it happen." Terrence said that they are important to the church and that the church is important to them. Some of the high school students run the church's media ministry, which he said has been invaluable. He said that before two students took charge of the media ministry, others were just "messing that stuff up" and he likes seeing the students "run to the church just to get back there (where the equipment is) and make sure it's A-OK." When asked what he has done to strengthen the church, Terrence said:

> I could easily say, "It was God," but that still wouldn't be answering the question. What I believe is at the heart of it is the same thing that's at the heart of my teaching experience with students. You have to care about the people. At the heart of anything is the people. That's that. When people see that you care about them, that you've got their back, really, that's what ministry is supposed to be about.

When Terrence began preaching as a young man, he was affiliated with a group of African American preachers who would preach at different churches of various denominations, including Baptists, Pentecostals, and Disciples. One Sunday, he was sent to a Disciples of Christ church to preach, and the church leaders appreciated his preaching. They invited him back, and eventually he became their pastor, serving that church ten years. When he began there, he was working in a factory. Then he enrolled in college: "I studied, and I studied, and I got my degree. ... I became a history teacher, football coach, basketball coach, and softball coach. I was enjoying myself doing those things. ... I was the last teacher to leave (at night) and then go teach Bible study, go home, and grade papers."

While pastoring, he enrolled in a program of theological education and training for ministers offered in his region. He completed the program and eventually was ordained. As he looks toward the future and his retirement, he encourages the church to invest in leaders for the future. After all, he said, "when you call someone to be a pastor, you really need to know who you're putting there. ... They might stay for a long time."

Pastor Sue began serving in a bivocational arrangement with Stone Ridge Christian Church, a predominantly white congregation, in her seventh year as their pastor. Sue loves the sense of community in the small town where Stone Ridge is located. The church has been a leading presence in the community for decades, and yet its membership is aging. The church is proud of its beautiful and well-maintained historic building.

Sue said it was pretty clear from the start of her ministry with Stone Ridge that money could become a problem. The church often had to dip into its savings to make ends meet. Sue said, "Every year when we were planning for the next budget cycle I would say, 'I'd rather you just let me know when my salary becomes a hindrance to the ministry of the church.'" By their seventh year together, she could see it was time to do something. She broached the topic again and proposed she become bivocational. The church members agreed to help figure out how to do that.

Both Sue and the church were thankful that a full-time position that fit with Sue's sense of vocation became available fairly quickly. As Sue began her new position in higher education administration at a school within a reasonable commute, her work at the church had to be curtailed to leave space for her new job. The people of the church "stepped up." Sue said: "They are protective of me and my time. Sometimes we're at a meeting and [someone says], 'Well, somebody needs to do this.' And I just sit there. ... It's not going to be me. Before, I might have jumped in to try to 'save the day' or something." For Sue and Stone Ridge, making the adjustments nudges all of them to review how they do things; they were used to doing things the "old way" with the minister trying to do it all. Yet here they are, putting their heads (and hearts) together to make it work.

WORDS OF WISDOM

Make Planning a Priority

It may go without saying: thinking ahead and making plans help bivocational ministers address challenges related to time. Many of them are serious about planning; they know it helps them to accomplish what's most important and to do so with less stress.

Many were eager to share with me what works best for them. They place the highest-priority work first as much as possible to make it less likely they will face significant time crunches.

Several bivocational ministers report using what they consider an effective weekly plan of action: making Sundays a full "church day." Those who do this usually concentrate their attention on worship leadership, teaching, and pastoral visits. Several also explained how they look ahead to the next Sunday and make sure they have settled on the next week's scripture and sermon topic by the end of the day on the previous Sunday. One minister reported that she works at least eight hours each Sunday because her other employment is full time and keeps her busy Mondays through Fridays. For her, Sundays involve leading worship and preaching in the morning, visiting with church members, as well as significant planning for next Sunday's worship. That administrative work includes drafting the next week's order of worship, sending emails to lay leaders who are involved, and getting a good start on the sermon. She usually finishes the plans for worship on Monday then works on the sermon throughout the week. Sunday worship is a top priority for her, and this work schedule helps her reach the end of the week with a sense of accomplishment and avoiding unexpected time crunches exacerbated by not planning ahead.

In addition to helping them accomplish their own goals, ministers also stated that thinking ahead and making plans helps "how" they work with others in congregations. These plans include being thoughtful about setting boundaries for what they are willing and unwilling to do. One bivocational minister who served in several congregations outlined three things he has always tried to do: (1) leave the worship bulletin preparation to someone else, (2) establish a weekly schedule of his availability and share it with the congregation, and (3) set aside a space at home to work on sermons. He said these boundaries helped him develop strong weekly habits that worked for him. Another minister described how he asked people to call him to make appointments for visits rather than holding "drop-in" office hours at the church building. Each Sunday he invited everyone to make appointments, and he included the invitation and his contact information in printed materials. While he received some pushback at first, he explained why he thought it was the best way for everyone involved to set aside the needed time. It turned out to work well after people had time to change their habits. Other ministers, several of whom were teachers, summarized "Plan B's" they established with lay leaders for pastoral care emergencies that emerge while they are at work.

Often the plans ministers make about how to allocate time depend on ministry priorities. Most weeks include administration (e.g., phone calls, texts, writing, sending emails), prayer, preaching (and sermon preparation), teaching (and lesson preparation), leading worship (and preparation), visiting people, and attending meetings. How much time is spent on each facet of ministry may vary week by week, depending on priorities. Something may emerge one week, such as a pastoral care emergency, and its emergence shifts what a pastor considers most important that week. Priorities are also influenced by the liturgical season, such as the always busy Holy Week. In addition, congregational priorities affect the way ministers plan their work.

Rachel McDonald, a United Church of Christ bivocational minister who writes the blog *My Other Job,* offers three different configurations of how she organizes a twenty-hour work week to accomplish ministry responsibilities. She uses colorful pie charts to illustrate each configuration, which reflects a different priority for congregational ministry: "outreach first," "balanced basics," and "preaching priority." For instance, her "outreach first" pie chart shows that she spends five hours on "community engagement" and two hours on "sermon writing." She notes that in the "outreach first" congregational setting members are satisfied with simple worship because of their emphasis on outreach to the community. In contrast, her "preaching priority" pie chart shows ten hours on "sermon writing" and zero hours on "community engagement" because in this setting the "congregation is seeking a preacher above all else." Her three configurations illustrate how ministry priorities in congregations affect the ways ministers might plan. Within all three settings she reminds us that bivocational ministry requires "the ability to notice things that need to get done [but] not do them sometimes."[26]

---

[26] Rachel McDonald, "Twenty Hours," *My Other Job*, February 5, 2024, https://myotherjob.substack.com/p/twenty-hours.

By looking ahead and planning in advance, ministers also help lay leaders collaborate better with them. For instance, some ministers stated that they use the three-year lectionary or develop longer-term sermon series to help them think further ahead about what they will be preaching. By doing this and sharing their preaching plans several months in advance, they help lay leaders consider how to plan creatively around preaching topics and scriptures. When ministers plan further ahead, in preaching or in other facets of ministry, their foresight supports shared ministry as people in the church are able to "mark their calendars" and feel less rushed in determining how to lead, participate, and support.

When ministers invest time in planning, it pays off for them and their congregations. They help pace themselves, accomplish what is most important, and structure how they work with others. Such advance planning improves opportunities for the kind of collaboration within congregations that supports shared ministry.

Reserve Time for Rest and Well-Being

"I'm worried a little about his stress level," said the spouse of one bivocational minister. "His brother recently had a heart attack, and he's working really long days." Those people who are closest to bivocational ministers often see they need rest, perhaps before they see it themselves. Even when ministers themselves finally recognize the need, time frequently slips away, they become caught up with important tasks, and needed rest falls by the wayside. Unfortunately, ministers can fall into unhealthy habits of letting vacation days pile up unused or working on their days off. It is important to their health and well-being to interrupt such a pattern by integrating rest and well-being into their lives on a regular basis. What that rest looks like varies for each minister, depending on factors related to their ministry context and other employment.

When ministers find a rhythm for their lives that includes rest and contributes to their well-being, they are following a pattern of work and rest that mirrors biblical wisdom. Many refer to such rest as "Sabbath," even when it is not a full day of rest. Sometimes it is scheduled time, as the weekly Sabbath, established and blessed by God (Gen. 2:1-3) and included in the commandments given to the people of Israel (Ex. 20:8-11; Deut. 5:12-15). At other times it is "time off" taken at different points in life, echoing the way Jesus stepped away for prayer and rest (Matt. 14:13; Mk. 1:35, 4:36, 6:46; Lk. 5:16, 6:12; Jn. 4:6) and encouraged his disciples to rest after a busy day (see Mk. 6:31). In Matthew 11:28 Jesus says to believers, "Come to me, all you that are weary and are carrying heavy burdens, and I will give you rest." Scripture reminds us that it is wise to reserve time for rest as part of a well-ordered and creative life and to take opportunities for rest along the way.

Some ministers find success in reserving time for rest by putting vacation days on their calendars and blocking out "time off" each week. For bivocational ministers, this may require some coordination if they need to consult other employers beforehand to schedule vacations or weekly time off. Once scheduled, such time off needs protection. Protecting this time is less challenging for ministers when they serve congregations that have reasonable expectations of them and respect for the boundaries of "time off." It is likewise less challenging to protect when congregation members are conscientious of the minister's schedule and look to elders or other lay leaders for leadership when ministers are not available, such as when the need for a funeral arises.

While rest is generally understood as time "away" from work, it also appears that resting and taking breaks help all of us, including ministers, live and work better and more creatively. One familiar approach to time management, the Pomodoro Technique, includes breaks as a key element. Software developer Francesco Cirillo, who created the approach in the 1980s, states: "Breaks allow you to step away for a moment, recognize fatigue, and decide whether to stop or continue. ... Breaks make us more productive, and they don't involve any work." He explains that including breaks as key elements in the technique "generates positive tension" and encourages people to see the passage of time in a positive way.[27]

Many bivocational ministers reported that they weave habits of rest and renewal into daily life, resting and finding renewal without a fixed schedule. It is necessary for some because

[27] Francesco Cirillo, *The Pomodoro Technique: The Life-Changing Time-Management System* (London: Virgin Books, 2018), 140-45.

scheduling vacations or time off is difficult. This is particularly true of ministers who have hourly work with unpredictable schedules or nighttime shifts, those who hold down more than one part-time job, and those whose work frequently entails travel. They find ways to replenish their energy when they are away from work by sharing meals and spending time with friends, neighbors, and family members, including children. They establish daily rituals of renewal, such as praying and reading devotions every morning, taking a morning or evening walk, caring for pets and wild animals, and reviewing the day at its end. One minister spoke at length about how important it is for him to spend time every day with the dogs that are part of his family. He said, "I have a better outlook on life the more time I spend snuggling with the dogs." Daily activities have the capacity to bring great peace and joy to life. Many mentioned hobbies or recreational activities that help them, including dancing, cooking, creative writing, fishing, gardening, hiking, journaling, playing games, and personal reading.

Some of the most stubborn obstacles for making rest and well-being a priority are rooted within ministers themselves. Ministers often find it difficult to say "no" and deal with the discomfort that comes with saying it. According to Kirk Bryon Jones, ministers may be reluctant or resistant to making rest and well-being a priority due to "overdone notions of indispensability and invincibility." When this is the case, he states, they subjugate "the most precious gift that God offers to each of us—personhood."[28] On the other hand, Jones asserts, when ministers accept that they are loved and valued by God because they are created in the image of God—and not because they are ministers or because they are productive—this knowledge empowers them to alter the way they value their own health and well-being.[29]

As a final note, let me say that ministers are wise to prioritize physical, mental, and emotional health as part of their well-being. It is important for them to develop habits of getting appropriate medical screenings and annual checkups, eating nutritious food, sleeping well, getting regular physical exercise, and seeing therapists and mental health professionals. That ministers pay

[28] Jones, *Rest in the Storm*, 34.
[29] Jones, *Rest in the Storm*, 36–37.

attention to their own mental health may be especially important for lessening stigmas around mental health and encouraging others to seek such care. They lead by example when they care for their own health and well-being.

Unwrap the Gift(s) of Community

"I'm a 'connector;' that's one of my gifts," said a bivocational interim minister in introducing herself to a congregation she was beginning to serve. She wanted to emphasize a few things with the congregation from the start. She had spent time discerning her spiritual gifts, and she was there to help them connect with their own, in the congregation and in their wider community. One of the wisest investments bivocational ministers can make is helping congregations see themselves as a community of people with God-given gifts meant to be used in shared ministry. Minister and church leader Kathleen Owens notes that the work of developing a comprehensive program of discernment of gifts in a local congregation involves a level of administration burdensome for many pastors, especially so for those who are bivocational. Yet she asserts that local pastors play the essential role in congregations of drawing attention to "the varieties of gifts that their members have to offer."[30] They are in a position to encourage individuals to discern their unique spiritual gifts—their interests, skills, motivations, their hopes and dreams, their sense of style, among other components—as "partners in the wondrous work of God,"[31] in their daily lives, in congregations, in the surrounding community, and in the wider world.

An essential component of this task is for ministers to get to know people in congregations really well. This means spending time with them, individually and in groups. Whether in Bible studies or conversations around sermons, over a cup of coffee or a plate of food at a church potluck, or over the phone, ministers need to talk with people and learn "who they are." While ministers indirectly learn some things "about" people, such as their names,

[30] Kathleen Owens, "Empowering the Full Body of Christ," *Bivocational and Beyond: Educating for Thriving Multivocational Ministry*, ed. Darryl Stephens (Chicago, IL: Atla Press, 2022), 211–23.

[31] Jean Morris Trumbauer, *Called and Created: Discovering Our Gifts for Abundant Living* (Minneapolis, MN: Augsburg Fortress, 1998), 18.

family relationships, and how long they've been part of the congregation, they really get to know people by talking with them. This is done best in "simple, honest conversation. Not mediation, negotiation, problem-solving, debate, or public meetings. Simple truthful conversation where we each have a chance to speak, we each feel heard, and we each listen well."[32] When ministers engage in such conversation, they demonstrate that they value people, provide better pastoral care, and gain insight into the many gifts that make up "who people are." Not everything ministers learn will be pleasant, but it will contribute to understanding individuals and the congregation. It strengthens ministers' relationships with people and touches all dimensions of their ministry, including praying, preaching, and teaching.

In their effort to get to know people, ministers are particularly blessed if they have congregational leaders and longtime members willing to help by making introductions and serving as companions when visiting people whom they may not have met on Sundays. When these leaders and longtime members become trusted companions in the work of knowing people well, they can better partner and work together to identify the gifts for shared ministry and provide care that people often need in church life. These conversations and relationships may lead to larger congregational discussions about a shared vision of the future.

Leadership that affirms and supports individuals and congregations discerning their own gifts is especially important in congregations shifting to bivocational arrangements due to decline. These congregations, which fit into the "A Sign of the Times" narrative about bivocational ministry, often face significant challenges. They find it difficult to imagine a ministry that depends less upon a minister with expertise than on a shared endeavor of the whole congregation. However, they've been searching for alternatives to ministry programs and approaches that no longer fit the congregation they are. When a minister helps them to recognize that vitality lies in shared and collaborative ministry, it can be an answer to their prayers. Ministers who help these

---

[32] Margaret Wheatley, *Turning to One Another: Simple Conversations to Restore Hope to the Future*, 2nd ed. (San Francisco, CA: Berrett-Koehler Publishers, 2009), 7.

congregations connect more fully with the God-given gifts already in their community provide leadership that is valuable.

Ministers can make first steps with simple actions to "unwrap" the presence of gifts within the congregation. One pastor initiated a simple action one year after Easter on a Sunday morning. When welcoming everyone at the beginning of worship, she invited them to bring some flowers from their yards for the next few weeks. The next Sunday someone remembered the invitation and brought in a vase of daffodils. The next Sunday someone else followed suit. Before too long different people in the congregation brought different flowers, in jars or vases, depending upon what was blooming. Whenever flowers showed up, the pastor mentioned them at the start of worship and acknowledged whoever had brought them. After worship the flowers went home with different people; often they were taken to church members who had not been able to come that Sunday. This continued into the summer. The next spring no invitation was needed; people had gotten the idea: they brought what flowers they had to share with the church and the broader community.

This "Backyard Bouquets" effort had been an invitation to community, one in which no money is spent and very little organization is required of the pastor. It was the simple self-organizing of community that reminded everyone of God-given gifts in their midst. In a larger congregation, with a staff of ministers, such a project might have been fully organized and managed for efficiency. However, when initiated by a bivocational minister, the community was left to organize itself. The simple action was only a beginning, but it was something replicable in other areas of ministry. Similar invitations in other areas of ministry have the potential to help congregations "tap into the gifts of others," even in connection with activities traditionally associated with "the minister," such as preaching. According to Shauna Hannan, Lutheran minister and professor of preaching:

> Preachers know that congregation members are not blank slates, but they often forget to tap their wisdom, expertise, and experience for biblical understanding and even sermon content. ... More often preachers turn to the

internet for illustrations, even though it is unlikely that such illustrations will strengthen relationships.[33]

There's much work to be done; good conversations and simple invitations to community are good places for bivocational ministers to invest energy and time and help them and their congregation discover how to serve God more fully.

Keep Learning, Unlearning, and Relearning

"We really learned to 'pivot.'" This was said by more than one pastor about leading congregations during the COVID-19 pandemic. Others would agree. When many congregations in the U.S. ceased in-person worship in March 2020, pastors were forced to learn new technology, unlearn how to lead worship, and relearn what people cared most about. The sudden and earth-shaking changes in 2020, which continue to have an impact years later, required ministers to make significant adjustments in the way they led their congregations—and lived their lives. Isn't this similar to what futurist Alvin Toffler predicted back in 1970? In his book *Future Shock*, he said that rapid technological change would mean that teaching students how to "learn, unlearn, and relearn" needed to be an integral part of education.[34] Bivocational ministers are wise to embrace the process of learning, unlearning, and relearning—and not simply in response to technological changes taking place around us. Many bivocational ministers can cite things they "wished they'd known" before "being bivocational."

As mentioned in the introduction, individuals take different educational routes to bivocational ministry. Some receive formal theological education and formation for ministry *before* becoming pastors, and others pursue it *afterward*. Some, for various reasons, do not receive formal theological education or formation for ministry at all, despite the advantages they offer. Whatever routes bivocational ministers take, they help themselves and their congregations when they intentionally pursue ways to grow in wisdom, skills, and technical knowledge. Many have

[33] Shauna Hannan, *The People's Sermon: Preaching as a Ministry of the Whole Congregation* (Minneapolis, MN: Fortress Press, 2021), 103.
[34] Alvin Toffler, *Future Shock* (New York: Random House, 1970), 356.

had to recognize knowledge gaps and be willing to broaden their perspectives so they can grow.

One bivocational minister spoke about a significant learning experience early in congregational ministry. He had decided to develop a shepherding program for the congregation, and he put together what he believed was an excellent plan. However, when he shared the plan, church leaders weren't persuaded. At first he thought he needed to revise the plan to develop something better suited. Then he realized why that wouldn't work: in his process of developing the plan he had neither collaborated with them nor inquired about their own sense of what was needed. He also realized the shepherding plan had disregarded the congregation's own patterns of caring for each other that they had been using successfully for decades. He had heard of similar programs working in other settings and had assumed one would fit there. His failure to plan *with* leaders had undermined any plan he would have developed *for* them.

Fortunately, this minister learned from this experience; he saw the plan's failure as an opportunity to develop into a better minister instead of being a sign he wasn't a good minister. He benefited from having a "growth mindset," a term developed by social psychologist Carol Dweck, to describe when individuals realize that their basic qualities "can be cultivated through their efforts, strategies and help from others."[35] Ministers with such a mindset understand that their wisdom, skill, and knowledge, like their spiritual practices and their relationship with God, can be cultivated and strengthened through effort, even when facing difficulties.

When things go wrong, as they frequently do, ministers learn by paying attention and being curious rather than focusing on hurt feelings. Seeking out feedback—inviting individuals to share what they observe—can be a practice that provides helpful insights from which ministers learn. According to minister and practical theologian Barbara Blodgett, feedback is "more valuable than praise" for ministers because of the insight that can be

---

[35] Carol Dweck, *Mindset: The New Psychology of Success* (New York: Ballantine Books, 2016), 7.

gained through the specifics of feedback.[36] Of course, listening and receiving feedback isn't easy; it demands that we be willing to listen to words that may not always be pleasant and to expend effort for personal and professional growth. Yet this is part of the work of learning. At the beginning of one of his prayerful poems, Howard Thurman, theologian and civil rights leader, says: "Give me the listening ear. I seek this day the ear that will not shrink from the word that corrects and admonishes."[37] His words seem almost shocking in a time when so many people avoid hearing words unless they are full of praise. Yet Thurman provides an important reminder to all whose goal is to learn: seek out words and experiences that provide insight into what needs to be done.

Seeking feedback also helps ministers to recognize when they have some "unlearning" and "relearning" to do. Some of what has been taught as "best practices" for ministry does not fit well in bivocational contexts. Likewise, what may have been accepted as "standard" expectations for ministers way back when turns out to be unrealistic for twenty-first-century bivocational ministers. In addition, much of what is used as indicators of thriving or successful congregational ministry (e.g., numbers in worship, size of congregation, ministry programs designed for targeted age groups) works well for larger congregations or those with fully funded ministers, but not so well for measuring congregational vitality in other contexts, including congregations with bivocational ministers. Bivocational ministers benefit from analyzing standard practices, expectations, and indicators of success and discovering what fits best in their bivocational contexts. Ministers may do much of this "unlearning and relearning" through conversations and observations around their experiences in ministry then reflecting on the outcome and meaning of those experiences. They also learn through their relationships and conversations with others, both in and outside congregations, including friends, colleagues, mentors, and authorities in various fields. The "learning labs" for bivocational ministers include their other places of employment as well as the church. And, in all this, ministers learn and grow through prayer,

---

[36] Barbara Blodgett, *Becoming the Pastor You Hope to Be: Four Practices for Improving Ministry* (Herndon, VA: Alban Institute, 2011), 24–33.

[37] Howard Thurman, *Meditations of the Heart* (Boston, MA: Beacon Press, 1981), 208.

meditation, study of scripture, and devotional reading. Even after formal courses of study, ministers need to keep learning, unlearning, and relearning. Ministry is full of challenges, and these challenges change over time.

None of Us Is Alone

Ministers sometimes express a sense of loneliness in ministry. The pressures of time and the various expectations placed upon them can lead them to feel isolated. When ministers are rooted in a stable relationship with God, that sense of loneliness can subside. As Romans 8:39 reminds all believers, nothing "in all of creation will be able to separate us from the love of God through Jesus Christ our Lord." Yet bivocational ministers also need reliable social support and connections with others as part of what researcher Matt Bloom calls their "ecosystem of wellbeing."[38] They need supportive relationships with all kinds of people—friends, family members, ministry and work colleagues, as well as people in their congregations and denominations. Both Pastor Terrence and Pastor Sue expressed appreciation for the ways their congregations supported them and collaborated with them. Even when the going gets rough, they know they have companions. They know that, then and always, others are praying for their success, cheering them on, and working with them to accomplish the work of the church, which itself is part of God's large mission in the world.

FOR REFLECTION AND DISCUSSION

1. What do you notice about Sue and Terrence's stories? What is similar and different about their experiences? What is significant about those similarities and differences?

2. What words of wisdom in this chapter surprise you and/or resonate with your experience?

3. What are some next steps that you or your congregation could take to help people recognize their gifts for ministry and feel confident that they are equipped to lead?

---

[38] Bloom, *Flourishing in Ministry*, 208.

CHAPTER 5

Money Matters: Finances and Supporting the Ministry

We're worried about "keeping the doors open and the lights on." More than one lay leader has made a comment like this. No matter whether they see bivocational ministry as "A Sign of the Times," "The Cutting Edge of the Future," or "The Way We've Always Done Ministry," money is a source of anxiety for many congregations with bivocational ministers.

Fieldview Christian Church's hundred-year-old clapboard building sits at an intersection of roads, surrounded by acres of farmland. Throughout its history, many bivocational pastors have led this predominantly white congregation. Its current bivocational pastor, Dirk, also works as a professional potter. He has been serving at Fieldview for more than seven years, and he appreciates how well lay leaders collaborate with him in their shared ministry, saying it embodies the priesthood of all believers. He also appreciates how the church does not have to worry about money because it "live[s] within [its] means" and keeps its focus on mission-based priorities. The church reviews financial reports and talks about plans at regular congregational meetings. At the end of 2019 the church had been considering an improvement to its building but changed plans after a thorough discussion. An elder summed up their reasoning: "It might make us happy, but it doesn't further God's ministry."

Because of that decision, the church had the funds it needed to weather the COVID-19 pandemic when it emerged in early 2020. Similarly, the church made the decision not to invest in equipment needed for livestreaming worship services when it closed its doors to in-person worship service that same spring, instead opting for Dirk to broadcast a Sunday morning worship service on Facebook from his home. That decision—and the broadcast worship—was well received. When the church reopened for in-person worship months later, it decided to keep the Facebook broadcast going. Dirk simplified the format a bit and moved it to an earlier time so he could make it to the church for the in-person worship. He said that the message or sermon on Facebook is now a shorter version of what he preaches in person at the church. This allows the congregation to connect with people outside the church while also focusing on the in-person worship service. He and church leaders are pleased with this practice; it fits well with their resources and furthers God's ministry and mission.

Dirk said another reason Fieldview doesn't need to worry about money is what he calls a "smart and generous" bequest the church received in the 1970s. A member of the church left a narrowly defined trust fund when she died, which provides annual interest income but no access to the principal. The annual funds received are deposited into a church account to be used for the minister's compensation. Thanks to this arrangement, the church has sufficient funds to compensate the minister even when costly problems emerge with the church building, such as the air conditioning failing, or when giving declines. This arrangement also frees the church to use weekly offerings and tithes to support the church's ministry and mission as well as the upkeep of church property. Dirk said this arrangement works well for the church and for him.

Pastor Letitia serves as a bivocational minister in an urban context. In addition to working outside the church, she is the lead pastor of two congregations in a shared ministry arrangement. Creative and complicated financial practices have developed as the relationship of the two congregations, Covenant City Christian Church and Unity Church, has matured.

Letitia is the founding pastor of Covenant City Christian Church. In 2014 she and the people who would become Covenant City were looking for a place to start their new church; that's when their relationship with Unity Church began. Unity was only using a portion of the large building they owned. When Covenant City looked around the building, they liked what they saw, and the two churches entered into a rental agreement. Unity was generous with the space; they welcomed Covenant City to use the fellowship and kitchen areas as well as all the worship space; they even set aside an office for Letitia. The members of both churches sat down and worked out the details, including when each church would use what parts of the building. One would hold Sunday worship at 10:00 a.m. and the other at 2:00 p.m.

It felt like a bit of an adventure for both congregations. As a new church, Covenant City was looking forward to using the space to worship and to planning some community development programs. As a declining congregation, Unity was hopeful they would make better use of their building and transform their ministry. The fact that this rental agreement was calling two very different congregations into a new relationship was not lost on anyone: the Covenant City church members were Black people of all ages, including children, and the membership of Unity were elderly white people.

Over time these people who shared the same building got to know each other better. By the end of 2019 they were sharing occasional fellowship time, programming, and special worship services. When the pandemic hit in 2020, Unity asked Letitia to serve as their pastoral care director while they looked for an interim pastor. During the pandemic Unity discontinued worship and Covenant City set up livestreaming with a worship leadership team using the sanctuary as home base. In 2022 they decided to draw closer together—not merging, but agreeing to share ministry in various ways, including worshipping together and calling Letitia their pastor.

In the early months of the shared ministry, they worked on how to manage their finances, which continued to remain separate. At first they held monthly meetings then moved to quarterly meetings to work on how to address the financial responsibilities they share. Covenant City uses online giving, but members of Unity use only cash or checks; they have two separate collection plates in Sunday worship. Most recently they have established a

Legacy Fund with its own bank account, and contributions from both churches are deposited into that account. Letitia also wrote some successful grant proposals that helped both congregations. "It's a work in progress," Letitia said. "You know, we just have to let the Lord decide how it's all going to finish itself." She said they are going slowly and trusting God as they move ahead.

SOME RECOMMENDATIONS CONCERNING FINANCES

Search Your Feelings

Many congregations, as well as individuals in them, have unexplored feelings about money. They may shy away from discussing money because they feel it's taboo or that it doesn't have anything to do with their spiritual lives. Yet in the gospels of Matthew and Luke, Jesus reminds us, "Where your treasure is, there your heart will be also" (Matt. 6:21; Lk. 12:34). What we do with our money is related to what is close to our hearts.

When individuals and congregations tackle a better understanding of feelings around money, they free its use for God's purposes. Unexplored feelings, such as fear or shame, can lead people to be secretive about money, cling tightly to it, or carry a burden of shame about the lack of it. While those of us in the church are to trust God foremost in our lives, burying our heads in the sand and thinking "God will provide" is not a faithful financial strategy.

Individuals and congregations alike may find it very helpful to examine their feelings by looking at their own money story, also known as a money autobiography. Feelings and habits about money are rooted in lessons learned throughout life (often unconsciously): from the families in which we grow up, the messages in the society around us, our experiences of losing and earning money, and what happens in the economic system operating around us. We also learn about money from what we experience in congregations: how ministers preach and teach about money, how leaders manage financial resources, how people give, and how the church supports mission and ministry. Thoughtful messages about money, both spending and giving, from ministers and other leaders help provide guidance to individuals in their own lives and to congregations as they develop priorities.

It is good to remember that money is something invented by human beings thousands of years ago as a tool to "facilitate the sharing and exchanging of goods and services among individuals and groups of people."[39] As a tool, congregations use money to pay what they owe (i.e., "paying the bills"), to support those whom they employ, and to fund the work of mission and ministry. When congregations thoughtfully and faithfully consider the priorities surrounding their use of money, they honor God and further God's mission.

Another way to view money is like water:

> Money flows through all our lives, sometimes like a rushing river, and sometimes like a trickle. When it is flowing it can purify, cleanse, create growth, and nourish. But when it is blocked or held too long, it can grow stagnant and toxic to those withholding or hoarding it.[40]

Many outside the congregations themselves benefit when churches feel free to allow money to flow through them and further God's mission.

Be Clear about the Church's Money

"Being clear" about money means a couple of things: it means being transparent about how church money is handled as well as communicating clearly about money matters within the church. Both are important in congregational life.

When congregations are transparent about how they handle money, the relationships of trust are strengthened. A good rule of thumb—actually a cardinal principle—is that handling the church's money is a multi-person effort: *no one should be handling the church money alone.* A quick review of the transparency of the congregation's money handling practices could begin with asking and finding the answers to questions such as:

---

[39] Lynne Twist, *The Soul of Money: Transforming Your Relationship with Money and Life* (New York: W.W. Norton and Co., 2017), 8.

[40] Twist, *The Soul of Money*, 102–103.

- How are the weekly offerings counted, recorded, and deposited?

- What kinds of internal controls are part of the way money is handled (online transactions, bank accounts, credit and debit cards, as well as the weekly offerings)?

- How are bank statements received, opened, and reviewed?

- How does the church make sure that bills are paid and legal forms are filed accurately and in a timely manner?

- What is the communication like with those who give to the church (e.g., do they receive receipts/contribution statements)?

- How are church financial records retained and kept secure?

Likewise, congregations are "being clear" when their communication about church money is open and honest. Regular and reliable financial reports help people in the pews understand how (their) church money is used. This may lead them to be more comfortable about contributing to the congregation because they know and trust the priorities of church spending and how the church's money is managed. It's part of that money and heart connection mentioned earlier.

When communication is not open, honest, or shared regularly, people are left with a lack of information, sowing doubt and mistrust. They may wonder about things like:

- What is the church's income (including the weekly offerings and other sources of income)?

- How much does the congregation have in the bank?

- What property or investments does the congregation have? (And what is the value of those assets)?

- What is the congregation's level of debt? (If there is debt, what are repayment plans and interest payments?)

- What expenses are expected in the next several months? (Are big projects coming, or are repairs needed to the building? What plans are being made to meet those expenses?)

- How much are employees paid, including the minister?

- How much is the church spending on different ministry priorities, such as community outreach or faith formation?

Helping people know about the church's financial situation is part of being good stewards of the church's resources. It helps church members appreciate the work done by those taking care of finances (church leaders or others who are hired to do this work). The reports don't need to be elaborate, but they do need a format church members can understand and trust.

This information is generally provided through financial reports such as written balance sheets, budgets, and income/expense statements. These kinds of reports are familiar to people with financial expertise, such as accountants. However, some churches do not have members with that kind of expertise. Resources are available to help congregations in this case.[41]

Sometimes information about the church's finances is held by only a few people and the rest of the congregations is "left out of the loop." Leaders may have reasons for holding back information about the church's finances. Some may lack confidence in their skill with financial matters or be anxious about the church's financial condition. And, unfortunately, we cannot ignore that some may have improper motives. For whatever reasons, when information about church finances is kept from those in the pews, it diminishes a sense of trust and the quality of decision-making in the church. It also may encourage the misconception that church property "belongs" to some in the church more than to others.

---

[41] Resources such as the *Minister's Tax & Financial Guide* and the *Church & Nonprofit Tax & Financial Guide* are offered without charge by the Pension Fund of the Christian Church (available to download for free at www.pensionfund.org) as well as the *Handbook for Treasurers of Christian Church (Disciples of Christ) Congregations* offered without charge from the Disciples Church Extension Fund (available to download at https://disciplescef.org/assets/docs/treasurers-handbook.pdf).

Being clear—open, honest, and transparent—about finances reflects the recognition that church property is held "in common" and does not belong to individuals. This is the closest most congregations in the twenty-first-century U.S. come to the idyllic portrait in Acts 4:32 of the earliest church, where all the believers were of "one heart and soul" and everyone held their "property in common."

Provide for the Pastor

How much to pay the pastor is a special concern for congregations with bivocational ministers and those considering calling one for the first time. It is important to reflect on what compensation is appropriate and fair. Compensation for bivocational ministers has great variation complicated by the reality that some have higher paying employment outside the church than others. According to the 2015 Lexington Theological Seminary survey of ministers, most often bivocational ministers receive a salary (88 percent), paid vacation (70 percent), housing (61 percent), and retirement funding (37 percent).

A variety of options are available to support ministers in terms of compensation, benefits, and allowances for ministry expenses (see checklist in Appendix B.) Options should be helpful as churches consider what to include in a ministry agreement with a new pastor or how they might enhance the support of their current pastor. Some options to consider help pastors without increasing their taxable income. Compensation and benefits provided to bivocational ministers are always contextualized, depending on factors such as a minister's other employment (its responsibilities, compensation, and benefits), how near they live to the church, the church's financial resources, and the expectations the church has of a minister. As mentioned in chapter 3's section about exploring expectations of ministers, it is beneficial to ministers and congregations to have a written ministry agreement. (See Appendix C for a sample of a contextualized ministry agreement.)

Almost all laypeople interviewed as part of the research project said they do not believe their bivocational ministers are paid enough. They look at what their ministers do and wish they could be paid more by the church. On the other hand, the ministers often expressed satisfaction with what they are paid. Yet it is important to note that ministers often are "reluctant to discuss financial issues with lay leaders at their churches" due to inner theological conflicts about being grateful to God—even when the needs of their families are not being met.[42] Conversations about compensation are best when they are honest, compassionate, and confirmed in writing.

One familiar practice in congregations with bivocational ministers is the giving of "love gifts." These gifts are ways congregations support ministers above and beyond their official compensation. Such gifts, which include monetary gifts as well as gifts of time and support, are an expression of care for the ministers. They may also be given as an indication that those in the congregations recognize that what they pay their ministers is insufficient for the time and energy they receive. The gifts include babysitting services, bouquets of flowers, and special monetary gifts collected to give to them at Christmas or the anniversary of their call to the church. Ministers also mention gifts of food, such as regular deliveries of fresh farm eggs, home-baked bread, Fruit-of-the-Month Club subscriptions, gift cards for coffee, and even excellent leftovers from potluck meals.

There are times when a congregation's pastor needs to look for employment outside the church. This need emerges for various reasons, including when the pastor:

- relocates to the community and looks for a job there

- loses or leaves a job and wants to remain bivocational

- needs to find a job because the church has decided to shift to a bivocational arrangement

These situations can be very stressful for pastors, and they provide opportunities for congregations to provide understanding and support. Packard Brown, an authority on the secular side of job searches for bivocational ministers, has spoken with people who have faced these challenges. In a conversation Packard and I had in February 2022, he recommended these pastors do an inventory of their own marketable skills. He also encouraged congregations

---

[42] Bloom, *Flourishing in Ministry*, 11.

to be willing to do the following when the pastor needs to find a job outside the church: (1) provide additional financial support for the pastor while they are unemployed and searching for a job; (2) serve as a network for contacting potential employers for the pastor; and (3) serve as a network of prayer.

Bivocational ministry should not be an excuse for congregations to pay ministers poorly or avoid accountability for proper stewardship of their financial resources. However, it does serve as a viable avenue for congregations when compensation and benefits provided to ministers are inadequate for their needs to support themselves and their households, including educating children and saving for retirement. According to Matt Bloom's *Flourishing in Ministry* research: "The pastor pay problem is thorny, complicated, and loaded with strong emotions. ... Everyone knows it is a problem, but few people appear willing to acknowledge and address it."[43] Congregations are called to hold these complicated conversations.

Keep the Bigger Mission in Mind

While the model of bivocational ministry contributes to financial stability, it's important for congregations to keep in mind what that improved stability supports in order to contribute to God's mission where they are located. The way they use their money should match what is at the heart of their ministry. For instance, when a congregation's priority is to "love God and neighbor" through vital worship and service to their community in the name of Jesus Christ, the flow of its money reflects that. Congregations benefit when they evaluate the way they spend money to determine the sustainability of their financial condition and the way their money contributes to God's larger ministry and mission.

Budgets can be a great tool for congregations because they are designed to help plan how money is used rather than simply keeping track of it. Many, but not all, use budget tracking systems to do this. According to the 2015 LTS survey, most bivocational ministers (81 percent) serve congregations that use written

---

[43] Bloom, *Flourishing in Ministry*, 11.

budgets. However, the smaller a congregation, the less likely it is to use a written budget. Only 28 percent of smaller congregations (those with fewer than fifty in weekly Sunday worship) use a written budget (whether their minister is bivocational or not). Using budgets or some other method, congregations are wise to analyze how well their spending reflects their ministry priorities.[44]

Sometimes the ways congregations use money can interfere with their intended ministry priorities. For instance, some congregations, particularly those that fit the "A Sign of the Times" narrative related to bivocational ministry, spend most of their money on the upkeep of property that is seldom used for ministry. Weekly offerings and tithes do not keep up with these expenses, and congregations may either turn to savings or allow the property to fall into disrepair. Or perhaps financial support for the upkeep of the building is less of a problem than its seldom use. Sometimes a congregation has aged and decreased in size until its "biggest problem is having a critical mass of people to carry on meaningful ministry."[45] In situations such as these, the flow of the money of the church is being blocked by the property rather than enabled to flow freely. In these cases, congregations need to analyze their financial situation and consider strategies to use their property for ministry. Varied options may be considered, including:

- providing space for ministry, including nonprofit organizations or other congregations
- partnering with other organizations to renovate the property for expanded ministry
- selling the property and purchasing or renting a right-sized space for their ministry
- merging with another congregation
- closing as a congregation and creating a legacy fund from the sale of the property

---

[44] Helpful resources related to congregational leadership of stewardship and financial practices are available online from the Center for Faith and Giving at www.centerforfaithandgiving.org.

[45] Len Eberhard, "Closing Rural Congregations," *Ending with Hope: Resource for Closing Congregations*, ed. Beth Ann Gaede (Bethesda, MD: Alban Institute, 2002), 101.

Pursuing these strategies involves grief. For many of these congregations, their buildings were constructed in a time when many were flocking to Sunday morning worship and educational activities. Congregations lament losses of membership and active ministry; they grieve that their building no longer matches their ministry. Yet that grief is accompanied by other emotions. When congregations move past denial about their situation and look openly and honestly at their financial options, they may sense relief when they address burdens they have carried for a long time; they even may discover a new sense of hope for the future.

In the New Covenant and Unity congregations referenced earlier in the chapter, grief is mingled with other emotions. Pastor Letitia recognizes it as members of Unity navigate many changes in their shared ministry with New Covenant. She related a conversation with Unity members about some of the changes when one of them spoke up and said: "If you all weren't here, we would have already closed."

Despite the emotional toll, it is better to begin the process than to delay it. When analysis and discernment are postponed, fewer options remain for viable ministry. As church buildings fall into disrepair from lack of use and deferred maintenance, their value diminishes for a congregation's active ministry, for their future legacy of hope, and for God's wider mission.

Any pastor leading a congregation considering these strategies needs support, even more so when they are bivocational. Analysis of a congregation's financial situation and discernment related to the use of its property are not tasks to be embarked on alone, even when ministers have relevant professional expertise. Regional ministers and other denominational leaders and consultants can provide helpful guidance for congregations and pastors in these situations.[46]

When congregations do not analyze their own financial condition and consider what is sustainable for the future, they can unintentionally hurt others. One bivocational minister explained

[46] Planning guides and other resources on related topics are available from the Disciples Church Extension Fund (www.disciplescef.org/resources/) and Christian Church Foundation (www.christianchurch-foundation.org/for-congregations/closing-congregations/).

how this happened when she took a lead position with a church. During the search process, the church leaders had offered her compensation and benefits that were enough for her needs. When she accepted the call, she packed up her belongings and moved to the state where the church was located. Once there, after a year as their lead pastor, it became clear to both her and the church leadership that the church would not be able to follow through on the compensation they had promised her. The church leaders apologized and said they had been hopeful; they had not meant to mislead her. However, she and the church were left in a difficult situation. Frustrated and low on funds, she began looking for another job while she and the church discerned how to move ahead. What a difference it would have made if this congregation had faced economic realities before calling this minister.

THE BOTTOM LINE

Money is a tool that should be used to facilitate God's mission. When congregations pay attention to how their money contributes to God's work where they are located, they enable it to flow rather than to become blocked or held too long. All congregations, like those led by Dirk and Letitia, face challenging decisions regarding the money with which they have been entrusted.

Thankfully, congregations have the capacity to attend to their finances faithfully, no matter the amount they have. Church leadership consultant Margaret Marcuson gives this reminder:

> The Holy Spirit is at work in all of our churches, in all the varied stages of the life journey of congregations, from church plants to those deciding it is time to close their doors. And the Spirit is at work in us, workaday church leaders who are trying our best to make decisions that are in the best interest of the church. [47]

Congregations and their leaders can approach the way they use money so the church uses it to do the work of God where they are located, no matter the size of their congregation, the size of their budget, or how long they have been operating as a church.

[47] Margaret Marcuson, *Money and Your Ministry: Balance the Books While Keeping Your Balance* (Portland, WA: Marcuson Leadership Circle, 2014), 11.

FOR REFLECTION AND DISCUSSION

1. Reflect about your own experiences with money. What influences can you identify that affect your feelings and/or habits connected with money?

2. What do you notice about how money plays a role in the congregations where Dirk and Letitia are pastors? What assumptions about money might contribute to difficulty in discussing finances in those congregations?

3. What is one step you or your congregation could take to allow money to flow through you and to support God's work more fully where you are located?

CONCLUSION

"It is a wonderful balance if you have a congregation that will work with you." These words, stated by Pastor Arvell (in chapter 3), reflect the feelings of many bivocational ministers. Such ministers are hopeful for the future of bivocational ministry. Like others with long-term experience in congregations that know "how to make it work," they see the increased attention to the way they've been doing ministry as a promising sign for the future. They would like to see more recognition of bivocational ministry as a viable and sustainable model of ministry. They would like to see better support for it as a model so it can thrive more fully. They see expanded recognition and support as increasingly important when congregations are transitioning to the model from one where the pastor has been working solely in the congregation. They also realize it is not appropriate for every congregation; no one model of ministry is. Yet they value it and would like to see it more fully recognized and supported.

Reflecting on their own experience, bivocational ministers paint portraits of bivocational ministry as deeply connected to the congregation and the congregation to their community.

Others raise concerns because of the toll it takes on ministers and congregations when it isn't working well.

GOD IS AT WORK IN BIVOCATIONAL MINISTRY

God is at work through the countless ministers who use their gifts more fully in bivocational settings.

Bivocational ministers not only influence others within the church itself; they also extend their influence outside the church. Many embrace a broad sense of serving God in the church and world. One minister recalled this from her own life when she told how influential it was to see a minister who also worked in an "ordinary" job. When she looked at that person, it helped her see that God could call her, an "ordinary" person, into ministry. Through their other employment, they also influence people who may never walk through the doors of a church building. A minister who earned money driving a taxi for several years recounted that people in the back seat of his taxi seemed willing to talk openly to him, whereas people in the church sometimes were more hesitant. In both settings he tried to be a good listener.

God is at work through the dynamic re-alignment of ministry implicit within the bivocational ministry model.

The hymn lyrics "Don't exalt the preacher, don't exalt the pew"[48] remind us that in the church no one should "lord it over" another. Ministers and "those in the pew" should work collaboratively rather than competitively. Equalized power relationships are promoted through bivocational arrangements because, with other sources of employment income, ministers do not depend entirely on the congregation for their livelihood. Both ministers and lay leaders indicated that this change also reduced the tendency to think of congregations as "employers" who hired ministers to "do ministry" for them. This re-alignment encourages both a sense of financial independence of ministers and congregational responsibility for ministry.

God is at work through the way the model expands participation of laity in the church.

Because bivocational ministers take on less responsibility for ministry in congregational life, laypeople take on more. When given a nudge to serve in new ways, many discover they have gifts for ministry and often find a new love for service. The need for—and emphasis on—lay leadership in contexts of bivocational ministry means that believers are invited more deeply to sacred service in the church, which builds up the body of Christ. When more laity recognize their capacity for ministry, both individuals and congregations grow stronger and serve God more faithfully.

---

[48] *African American Heritage Hymnal* (Chicago, IL: GIA Publications, 2001), Hymn 547.

God is at work through the ways bivocational ministry enables congregational viability in diverse and challenged contexts.

God created a world full of diversity, from microbes to mammoths, and continues to work creatively through that diversity. Many congregations that appear insignificant in size or location provide important and transformative ministry in both word and deed. Just as the apostle Paul found his weakness to be a sign of his own apostleship, these congregations see God working in them despite their weakness. Without the model of bivocational ministry, these congregations would be without pastoral leadership due to their inability to provide adequate financial support for a minister. The bivocational model enables these congregations to continue and expand ministry in the diverse set of communities where they are located.

Ministry thrives with support—and bivocational ministry thrives with more support.

When bivocational ministers are supported and encouraged, they can enrich the church and the world. And they need more support and encouragement. Some have become bivocational ministers despite significant challenges along the way. Some have served diligently while being overlooked and marginalized due to the dominant presence of the "Standard Model" of full-time ministry and the "full-time bias." Providentially, many have persevered nonetheless. Many were led to congregations and ministries where they could serve faithfully. God works through them powerfully when they bring their own experiences to bear in service to God in Christ's name.

Congregations that have long-term experience with the model have learned how to make it work, figuring it out almost in a "do-it-yourself" style. They have, over time, developed resilient traditions of collaborative ministry, contextual patterns of leadership development, and various practices that provide support when ministers also work outside the church. Sometimes the development process has involved times of trial and error. I imagine this process of ministers and laypeople discovering ways to support one another as a "living trellis" where they grow and mature in service to God where they are located. In this, they resemble the "Three Sisters" garden,[49] in which corn, beans, and squash grow together in mutually beneficial relationships and create an ecosystem beneficial for them all. When congregations and their ministers develop such an ecosystem, they also bear fruit for ministry in their communities and serve God more fully.

Yet even though congregations with bivocational ministers are finding ways for bivocational ministry to thrive, they would benefit from additional support. Their leaner staffing and smaller numbers mean that they would benefit from a support system that goes beyond ministers and congregations figuring out "how to make it work" on their own. While it's not clear how a trellis of support for bivocational ministry would look, it would look different from the support that was designed primarily with the full-time ministry model and larger congregations in mind. After all, a tomato cage looks different from the trellis designed to support a rambling rose, bivocational ministry has its own needs for support. Many of their needs cause us to raise good questions, with implications for ministry organizations and denominations. For example:

- How might retirement savings programs be adapted for bivocational clergy?

- How could recognition of the value of the bivocational ministry model be expanded?

- What adjustments could help make the "Search and Call" system fit better with bivocational arrangements?

- How could helpful conversations centered on compensation and expectations for bivocational ministers be encouraged?

- How might "right-sized" resources be developed to help smaller congregations without a full ministry staff?

---

[49] In the "Three Sisters" garden, practiced for thousands of years by different tribal people in North America, corn, beans, and squash are planted as companions. The stalks of the corn plant become the trellis for the beans, the beans add nitrogen to the soil, and the leaves of the squash shade the base of the plants, helping moisture remain in the soil and suppressing the growth of weeds.

- How can investments be expanded to strengthen lay leadership and "shared ministry"?

- What else?

However a trellis of support for thriving bivocational ministry ends up looking, it holds the promise of strengthening congregational ministry with other models of ministry as well. In the mixed ecology of the twenty-first-century ministry landscape, expanded and redesigned support that helps congregations facing the kinds of challenges described in this book would provide support beneficial to other models of ministry as well.

During the COVID-19 pandemic, the mantra "We're in this together" was heard repeatedly in Kentucky and in many other places. The governor of Kentucky, Andy Beshear, repeated the phrase "We're in this together, and we'll get through this together" during his regular broadcasts. He recognized that when facing challenges, people could be tempted to respond by turning inward and away from others. In a time when pandemic mandates and school closings called for physical "social distancing," Beshear engaged in the important habit of using words and actions to encourage connectedness and compassion. In addition to his words, he lit the Governor's Mansion with green lights each evening to honor Kentuckians who had died that day and encouraged others in the state to do the same. The "green lights for compassion" began appearing all over the state, signaling people to "go ahead" and show that they were standing together when facing that challenging time of grief and division.

The church also functions better when we share the sense that we are all in this together. As congregations and ministers work to thrive together, it might be a good time to light some green lights, too. We can signal that we're also standing together and ready to go ahead and support ministry that thrives in the twenty-first-century landscape. Just as in the scriptural image of the cultivated field in 1 Corinthians 3:5–9, cultivation is taking place in a diverse ecosystem. In various ways, God empowers the growth, with many congregations as places of growth and ministers and laypeople alike planting the seeds and watering the crops.

BIBLIOGRAPHY

Adichie, Chimamanda Ngozi. "The Danger of a Single Story." TED Talks. Filmed July 2009. Video, 19:16. https://www.youtube.com/watch?v=LmjKUDo7gSQ.

African American Heritage Hymnal. Chicago: GIA, 2001.

Bentley, Kristen Plinke. "Perspectives of Bi-Vocational Ministry: Emerging Themes in Bi-Vocational Ministry Research at Lexington Theological Seminary." Lexington Theological Quarterly 48 (2019): 115–51. https://lextheo.edu/wp-content/uploads/2021/09/j-4-Perspectives-of-Bi-Vocational-Ministry.pdf.

———."Pitching Our Tent with Bivocational Ministry." In *Bivocational and Beyond: Educating for Thriving Multivocational Ministry*, edited by Darryl Stephens, 111–31. Chicago: Atla Open Press, 2022. https://books.atla.com/atlapress/catalog/view/82/206/859.

———."Stability Amidst Turbulent Times: the Benefits of Bi-Vocational Ministry." *Colloquy Online,* Association of Theological Schools (May 2019). https://www.ats.edu/files/galleries/stability-amidst-turbulent-times-the-benefits-of-bi-vocational-ministry.pdf.

Blodgett, Barbara. *Becoming the Pastor You Hope to Be: Four Practices for Improving Ministry.* Herndon, VA: Alban Institute, 2011.

Bloom, Matt. *Flourishing in Ministry: How to Cultivate Clergy Wellbeing.* Lanham, MD: Rowman and Littlefield, 2019.

Chaves, Mark, Holleman, Anna, and Hawkins, Mary. National Congregations Study: Congregations in 21st Century America. 2021. https://sites.duke.edu/ncsweb/files/2022/02/NCSIV_Report_Web_FINAL2.pdf

Cirillo, Francesco. *The Pomodoro Technique: The Life-Changing Time-Management System.* London: Virgin Books, 2018.

Culpepper, Lisa. *Together Is Better: How Small Membership Churches Fulfill God's Missional Call through Partnerships.* Independently published, 2021.

Diehl, William. *Ministry in Daily Life: A Practical Guide for Congregations.* New York: Alban Institute, 1996.

Dweck, Carol. *Mindset: The New Psychology of Success.* New York: Ballantine Books, 2016.

Eberhard, Len. "Closing Rural Congregations." In *Ending with Hope: Resource for*

Closing Congregations, edited by Beth Ann Gaede. Bethesda, MD: Alban Institute, 2002.

Edington, Mark. *Bivocational: Returning to the Roots of Ministry.* New York: Church Publishing, 2018. http://www.bivocational.church/.

Handbook for Treasurers of Christian Church (Disciples of Christ) Congregations. Revised December 2016. https://disciplescef.org/assets/docs/treasurers-handbook.pdf.

Hannan, Shauna. *The People's Sermon: Preaching as a Ministry of the Whole Congregation.* Minneapolis, MN: Fortress Press, 2021.

Jones, Kirk Byron. *Rest in the Storm: Self-Care Strategies for Clergy and Other Caregivers.* 20th anniversary ed. Valley Forge, PA: Judson Press, 2021.

Jung, Shannon. *Rural Ministry: The Shape of the Renewal to Come.* Nashville, TN: Abingdon, 1998.

Lartey, Emmanuel. *In Living Color: An Intercultural Pastoral Care and Counseling.* 2nd ed. Philadelphia, PA: Jessica Kingsley Publishers, 2003.

Law, Eric. *The Wolf Shall Dwell with the Lamb: A Spirituality for Leadership in a Multicultural Community.* St. Louis, MO: Chalice Press, 1993.

MacDonald, Jeffery. *Part-Time Is Plenty: Thriving without Full-Time Clergy*. Louisville, KY: Westminster John Knox, 2020.

McDonald, Rachel. "Twenty Hours." *My Other Job*, February 5, 2024. https://myotherjob.substack.com/p/twenty-hours.

Marcuson, Margaret. *Money and Your Ministry: Balance the Books While Keeping Your Balance*. Portland, WA: Marcuson Leadership Circle, 2014.

Owens, Kathleen. "Empowering the Full Body of Christ." In *Bivocational and Beyond: Educating for Thriving Multivocational Ministry*, edited by Darryl Stephens, 211–23. Chicago, IL: Atla Open Press, 2022. https://books.atla.com/atlapress/catalog/view/82/212/865.

Theological Foundations and Policies and Criteria for the Ordering of Ministry of the Christian Church (Disciples of Christ) updated 5/8/2014. https://cdn.disciples.org/wp-content/uploads/2014/07/06162557/TFPCOM-Final.pdf.

Thurman, Howard. *Meditations of the Heart*. Boston, MA: Beacon Press, 1981.

Toffler, Alvin. *Future Shock*. New York: Random House, 1970.

Trumbauer, Jean Morris. *Called and Created: Discovering Our Gifts for Abundant Living*. Minneapolis, MN: Augsburg Fortress, 1998.

Twist, Lynne. *The Soul of Money: Transforming Your Relationship with Money and Life*. New York: W.W. Norton and Co., 2017.

Wheatley, Margaret. *Turning to One Another: Simple Conversations to Restore Hope to the Future*. 2nd ed. San Francisco, CA: Berrett-Koehler Publishers, 2009.

What Do You Expect? Worksheet of Ministry Expectations

Here is a list of ministry tasks for congregations to review with three questions in mind:

1. What do you expect the minister to do?

2. How necessary is it for the minister to do that?

3. Who else in our congregation has the gifts to do that?

With your own congregation in mind, review the following list of tasks. The first time you review the list, mark an "M" (for "Minister") next to those tasks you expect your minister to do. Then revisit the list. This time, mark an "N" next to items you think are necessary for the minister to do and a "C" next to those items others in the congregation could do. If there are ministry tasks left off this list that fall into your expectations, add them to the bottom of the list with the appropriate mark (M, N, or C) next to them.

1. Leading the congregation in weekly Sunday morning worship services

2. Preparing and delivering sermons in weekly Sunday worship (including holiday weekends)

3. Preparing and delivering a children's message in Sunday worship

4. Working with musician(s) in the selection of music for worship

5. Developing the format and content of the worship service

6. Participating with the elders at the Lord's Supper in Sunday worship

7. Preparing an accurate Sunday worship bulletin

8. Preparing laypeople for leadership in various parts of worship

9. Preparing and leading special services or activities (such as Ash Wednesday, Maundy Thursday, Good Friday, Easter Sunrise, Christmas Eve, Night Watch)

10. Visiting church members who cannot attend worship (such as those in a hospital, nursing home, or at home) and determining how often this should happen

11. Providing support and comfort to church members in need

12. Conducting funerals for church members (including visiting bereaved family members as soon as possible and meeting with them to plan the funeral)

13. Conducting weddings for church members

14. Holding office hours at the church and deciding how many hours per week

15. Communicating with the congregation via email, newsletters, social media, etc.

16. Being present for church events, including Vacation Bible School

17. Monitoring the financial health of the congregation

18. Aiding the development of an annual budget for the church

19. Developing an annual stewardship program for the church

20. Serving as an ex officio member of church committees and boards

21. Ensuring accurate and timely submission of forms

22. Coordinating strategic long-range planning for the congregation

23. Organizing congregational fellowship activities

24. Developing a comprehensive youth ministry

25. Equipping lay leaders of the church

26. Leading spiritual development activities for members of the congregation

27. Teaching weekly Bible studies

28. Conducting classes for youth and adults in preparation for baptism

29. Teaching new members classes

30. Identifying those with gifts for ministry

31. Appointing deacons and elders of the church

32. Attending local community events, such as high schoolsporting events

33. Being active in the local ministerial association

34. Participating in regional or denomination-wide events

35. Other:

(This activity sheet is not meant to be interpreted as suitable for a minister's job description.)

APPENDIX B

Checklist: Compensation Options for Ministers

This list includes common components of what congregations provide ministers through financial and housing compensation, benefits, and expense allowances.

Compensation

- Salary
- Housing** (allowance and/or provision of church-owned parsonage)

Benefits

- Social Security offset (ministers pay 15.3 percent of salary and housing allowance for Social Security)
- Employer contributions for health care (contributions to health savings account or health reimbursement account)
- Employer contributions for retirement** (contributions for the pension plan or tax-deferred retirement account)
- Employer-funded insurance** (i.e., health, life, workers' compensation, and liability)
- Holidays*
- Paid vacation* (most bivocational minsters surveyed reported two to four weeks per year)
- Paid sick leave*
- Paid parental and family leave*
- Paid educational leave and/or renewal/sabbatical leave*

Allowances for Ministry Expenses (Accountable Reimbursement Plan**)

- Church funds set aside for reimbursement of minister's professional expenses, such as automobile mileage and tolls; registration, overnight lodging, and meals for conventions and assemblies; continuing education; books and subscriptions; and other professional expenses

* Paid time off provides significant support for bivocational ministers' well-being.

** If handled according to IRS specifications, these items do not increase a minister's taxable income. Always consult with a tax professional for specific situations.

This checklist is adapted from pages 29–43 of the *Handbook for Treasurers of Christian Church (Disciples of Christ) Congregations* (at https://disciplescef.org/assets/docs/treasurers-handbook.pdf). More in-depth information about these items can be found there.

APPENDIX C

Sample of a Bivocational Ministry Agreement

Each ministry agreement with a bivocational minister has a context. It considers both the minister's unique personal situation, including their other employment, along with the congregation's needs, resources, and ministry priorities. This sample agreement is for a minister who works twenty hours for the church each week while also employed full time in a position with a business in a nearby community. The minister commutes twenty minutes from her home to the church. Health insurance for the minister and her household is entirely funded through her other employment.

Fairfield Christian Church

MINISTRY AGREEMENT

The following items represent the agreement that formalizes the relationship between Fairfield Christian Church and called minister, Rev. Roberta Brown.

This agreement is subject to the approval of the Fairfield Christian Church board and congregation.

I.   Fairfield Christian Church of [Hometown, STATE] agrees to call Rev. Roberta Brown as their minister.

II.   Termination by either party shall be given 60 days in advance of the conclusion of the ministry.

III. The minister will look to the board chairperson for oversight and general guidance and be an active, non-voting member of the board.

IV. The elected elders of the congregation will serve as a Pastoral Relations Committee to support the minister, conduct an annual review of the ministry agreement, and address concerns that may arise.

V. <u>Rev. Roberta Brown</u> will be present with the
    congregation as its pastor for the following days and/or
    hours each week:

    Sunday mornings for worship and ministry activities

    Wednesday evenings for teaching activities

    10 hours in home office

    As needed for special services, functions, and
    emergencies

    Total of 20 hours per week

VI. The minister will, in the time agreed upon in item
    IV, conduct Sunday worship services and collaborate
    with church leadership to provide pastoral care to
    individuals and households; offer administrative
    leadership and guidance to leadership groups within
    the congregation; nurture members in their Christian
    faith; equip congregational leadership through
    mentoring, teaching, and providing resources; and
    address other congregational needs.

VII. Compensation, benefits, and allowances for the
     minister are:

     $— per year for salary

     $— per year for housing

     Social Security Offset (15.3 % of salary and housing
     allowance for Social Security)

     $— per year retirement contributions

     $— ministry expenses reimbursement (through the
     Accountable Reimbursement Fund)

     3 days of professional development per year

     0.5 sick days per month

     2 weeks of paid vacation for year 1

     3 weeks of paid vacation per year for years 2–4

     4 weeks of paid vacation per year for years 5+

     Renewal Leave Fund

The congregation's treasurer works with the minister to record vacation time, sick days, reimbursements through the Accountable Reimbursement Fund, and professional development days.

Unused sick days and vacation days will be carried over to the next year, and unused vacation (a maximum of four weeks) will be paid at the point of termination.*

Accountable Reimbursement Fund: The congregation will set aside $— each year for reimbursement of minister's professional expenses, such as automobile mileage and tolls; registration, overnight lodging, and meals for conventions and assemblies; continuing education; books and subscriptions; and other professional expenses. Unused reimbursement funds will not be paid to the minister at the end of the year nor be carried over to the next year.

Renewal Leave Fund: the congregation will contribute $— each month to a Renewal Leave Fund. Beginning in year 4, the minister may draw on those funds to reimburse renewal or educational uses. Funds may be used only to reimburse expenses approved by the elders and treasurer for the minister. Unused renewal leave funds will not be paid at the point of termination.

Signed: _____   _____
                  Minister   Church Officer

Date: _____